L.E.O.
THE TRUE STORIES
OF
LT. WAYNE COTES

Author
Wayne Cotes

Edited By
Denise Bohart Brown

Printed in the United States of America

Library of Congress Control Number: 2021904283
ISBN: Softcover   978-1-64908-902-1
         Hardback   978-1-64908-903-8
         eBook   978-1-64908-901-4

Republished by: PageTurner Press and Media LLC
Publication Date: 03/11/2021

To order copies of this book, contact:

PageTurner Press and Media
Phone: 1-888-447-9651
order@pageturner.us
www.pageturner.us

This book is dedicated to the men and women of my department specifically, and law enforcement in general. They are a hard-working and dedicated group of professionals doing a difficult and often thankless job in an exemplary manner.

Despite what you hear in the media about police officers, these law enforcement professionals are truly dedicated to protecting and serving their community. Every year they handle tens of thousands of calls for service, remain proactive in their approach to policing, and still find time to take low-income kids on various summer trips and give tirelessly to ensure those same kids have a great Christmas by donating their own money and time to buy presents.

At last count, they served some 600 families during the holiday season.

Thank you for the job you do. You are noble and courageous, and I am both honored and humbled to have served beside you.

A note about the cover. There are multiple overlapping meanings to the design I chose. LEO stands for Law Enforcement Officer. My birth sign also happens to be LEO and is represented by the lion. If you have ever been to the National Law Enforcement Memorial in Washington D.C. (and I would encourage anyone to do so), two lions stand guard over the memorial. The symbolism might be a bit much for some and that's ok, it meant something to me.

INTRODUCTION

This book was 27 years in the making. I started my law enforcement career in May of 1991 as a police officer for a municipal agency and then in 1993, I found the department I would call home for the next 25 years. It has not always been the smoothest road. I've made decisions along the way that have landed both my department and me in trouble. I've lost friends, including three in one day. I've been to too many homicide scenes, seen too many dead babies, and felt the heartbreak and sorrow of a community that has suffered too long from violence and apathy. Twenty-seven years has left more than its fair share of scars, physical and otherwise. In December 2017, I decided to hang up my gun belt and signed the papers that will lead to my full retirement.

When I first started in law enforcement, I used to call my parents to tell them about my week. My dad was comfortable with hearing about my entire week: the good, the bad, and the ugly. My mom.... not so much so. She didn't want to know about the foot pursuits through back yards going after men with guns, drugs, and histories of violence. She didn't want to hear about the homicide scene I was at earlier in the day or the car crash that took the life of a five-year old boy. Honestly, who can blame her? It isn't normal for people to be exposed to that toxicity day in and day out. What she did want to hear about was the funny, silly, and sometimes downright stupid things that happened to me during the week. For my mom, I started telling those stories.

One day, I was at my best friend's wedding reception and to kill some time, someone passes me a mic and asks me to tell a story to a room crowded with a hundred-plus people. To set the scene, we're at a club called Hide & Seek. It's a gay bar and my best friend's brother is an entertainer there. The club is a diverse mix of gay and straight, transvestites and non-transvestites, and young and old. I'm not a public speaker. Oh, I can get up in front of a room of 250-plus people and talk about crime trends and public safety initiatives, but this was different. I was expected to be entertaining.

I took a long pause, mostly to steady my breathing and calm the nervousness I was feeling. Then I started telling the story about the two men on the moped and to my surprise, people loved it, so I told another and even possibly a third before someone wrestled the microphone away from me so they could introduce the bride and groom.

After the wedding, my mom encouraged me to start writing down my stories before I forgot them. A few years later, someone created a blog for me to write my stories down in so that I could share them with friends and family. Friends and family shared my blog with people who shared it with other people and pretty soon, I was getting comments from people who lived in my city.

Then the day came when one of my officers was watching a movie of the adult variety. He was fond of a particular actress and decided to look her up and see what other movies she may have starred in. In doing so, he stumbled across a friend of mine who has the same name as the adult film actress. She also happens to be the one who created the blog for me. No, she isn't a porn star. She was however a red-haired librarian with a sexy sounding name. Right up this officer's alley so he clicked on her webpage and immediately recognized her as my friend. Then he saw a link to my blog and clicked on that.

By the time that I came in on Monday morning to conduct briefing, every officer in the Department had read the blog. To my surprise, they loved it. They wanted to be seen as human, capable of doing dumb shit, making mistakes, and having feelings like every other person on the planet, and they liked that I showed that through humor.

The blog still exists in its original format, though you'd have dig to find it. Here, in this book, I've done some editing, changed the names to protect the innocent and all of that. The stories themselves are all true (though with maybe a bit of embellishment to make them funnier) but, to the best of my recollection at the time they were written, they are accurate.

Some notes on the writing style: a lot of these stories were written at the time they happened so they're in the present tense even if they occurred 10-plus years ago. I also did not have these stories professionally edited. My editor is probably cringing right now. After reading my first book, *"Me, The World, and a Dog Named Steve,"* she offered her editing skills to me, mostly because my poor grammar, spelling and misuse of words drove her crazy (she has since finished editing this book and this was her response to my previous statement – "You're getting better though! And BTW, your grammar is not bad, and your spelling is generally fine [other than occasional typos] – it's more the wrong words and the punctuation that drove me crazy. LOL.")

I hope you enjoy these stories. If you have questions or comments, please feel free to email me at wayne.cotes@yahoo.com or you can visit my webpage at www.waynecotes.com and leave me a message there. Also, if you're interested in reading my adventure fiction novels, *"Me, The World, and a Dog Named Steve: The Mini-Expeditions,"* and *"Woden's Key: A Me, The World, and a Dog Named Steve Adventure,"* and my latest release, *"The Undying: A Me, The World, and a Dog Named Steve Adventure"* they are all available on Amazon in either paperback or ebook.

REPUTATIONS

When I was reassigned from Investigations to Community Policing, I was given my choice of the areas where I could choose to work. I narrowed it down to two choices, Pine Cone Court or Stadium Gardens.

Both properties were tough nuts to crack. There was a criminal subculture in both developments that ran deep and had gone on for several generations. The drug operation in the movie "New Jack City" was based on that of Stadium Gardens during its so-called "glory" days when one of the biggest drug dealers in my city's history was alive and running the show. Pine Cone Court was the hard of the hard – the true ghetto.

I balanced them out. Pine Cone Court was scheduled for demolition in another year so I figured that I didn't have time to build up a good rapport with the community so the true work of community policing could begin, so I chose Stadium Gardens as my stomping grounds.

I was attempting to cultivate a reputation for being firm but fair. I didn't allow my need to build up trust in the neighborhood dissuade me from performing my duties as a law enforcement officer. If confronted by one of the dealers I stood my ground, but I didn't hassle them if all they were doing was standing around; I told them it was safer for them to be in their "turf" with me around than it was for me to move them out into an adjoining area and have violence erupt.

One night I'm on foot patrol and come across a group of 20 to 30 guys involved in an illegal dice game. I walk up, and no one is moving.

One of older guys finally speaks up and asks me, "What you gonna do, Cotes? We all know you're out here alone. You can't stop us."

And damn it all if he wasn't right. I was alone. Now regarding stopping them, well, that remained to be seen. I walked off, back around the corner, stopped, drew my baton and turned back around. I then took off at a full run back around the corner, and straight at the group involved in the illegal dice game, waving my baton above my head and yelling at the top of my lungs.

There was momentary stunned silence and then frantic scrambling as people grabbed dice, money, and jackets and headed for the hills. One poor guy was spider crawling backwards across the ground to get away from me. Him, I cuffed.

From that point forward, whenever someone new would come into the area and start talking smack while I was attempting to identify them, the older guys would tell them, "Don't mess with Cotes, man, he's crazy as all fuck."

Not the reputation I wanted but it would do.

CREEPING

Roly was a little side street off of the 2400 block of 26th Avenue. There's only one way for a vehicle to get onto the 2400 block of 26th Ave., and that's off Logan Street. The dealers used to set up shop just north of Roly Court, at an apartment complex with more exits than a prairie dog colony.

Roly was a little side street off of the 2400 block of 26th Avenue. There's only one way for a vehicle to get onto the 2400 block of 26th Avenue, and that's off Logan Street. The dealers used to set up shop just north of Roly Court, at an apartment complex with more exits than a prairie dog colony.

At night, I would get onto Roly Court by making the turn from Logan onto 26th Avenue with my bright lights on. The effect was that anyone looking at my car would see nothing but bright lights and not the fact that it was a squad car. I could then make the turn onto Roly Court and enter the complex from the rear so that I was behind the drug dealers.

One night, as I parked my car, there was an older lady who was walking out of a house on Roly Court and saw me. We exchanged pleasantries and then she began to walk off down the street as I began to make my way through the complex.

I managed to get within five feet of a gate where the dope dealers were set up. I commence to watching, waiting to see if they'd make a deal, and looking to see where they are keeping their stash.

As I'm standing there monitoring, I hear the lady's voice, the one I had said hello to earlier, telling the dealers, "Five-0 (from the

3

popular TV series Hawaii Five-0, it's a street term for cop) is out walking around."

The dealers immediately jump back behind the gate, now on the same side as me, and start peeking down the street. (I feel like this needs a bit more descriptive to set the scene as to who is where – I don't want to complicate things, but what you are seeing clearly in your head is less clear in my head. I picture a gate that is closed, with you on one side looking through to the dealers on the other, so then I have a hard time picturing it when they "jump back behind the gate." Maybe mention that you are tucked in the shadows, or that the lady showed up on the other side of the gate, or something to draw the picture a bit better.)

From the shadows I tell them, "No need to look out there, I'm right here."

What ensued was like something from a Three Stooges movie. Both dealers jumped about three feet in the air, turned towards each other and tried to take off running but instead collided with one another. There was a great deal of hand slapping and pushing before either managed to recover well enough to take off running. By this time, I was laughing so hard I couldn't have pursued them even if I had something worth chasing them for.

IS IT A ROCK OR A ROCK!?

We were working a reverse buy/bust operation in conjunction with another police department. They were providing the sellers and the chase cars plus some arrest teams while we were providing additional arrest teams and the mobile command center for booking.

There's something to be said for working with members of other departments but it comes with its problems, too. For instance, even if my officers don't use their call signs, I know their voices and can tell who is who. The same can be said for the other department's officers – they know their people as well.

One suspect in a pickup truck rolls up to the undercover officers and asks to buy some weed. They promptly sell him some bunk (fake weed) and give the signal that the sale is complete. The chase car then starts to follow the suspect out of the area.

As the chase car is following the suspect, the officer in the chase car says over the air that the suspect pulled over to the side and was picking up a rock.

We were doing an undercover drug operation so when the chase man said that our suspect was picking up a rock, we assumed that he was purchasing rock cocaine.

As the arrest teams are attempting to get into a position where they can make an arrest, the chase officer is getting frantic over the air.

Chase officer: "Someone get up here quick, he's following me, and he's got a rock."

Unknown Officer: "Is this a rock or this a ROCK?"

Chase officer: "This is a ROCK and he intends on using it. If you don't get up here quick this is going to get ugly."

The emphasis makes it clear. Our suspect has a ROCK, as in a boulder, and is thinking of using it on our undercover chase guy. Check. That clarifies things now, doesn't it?

AND THE ACADEMY GOES TO... OR MELODRAMA ON THE GRASSY KNOLL

Officers were dispatched to a possible auto burglary in progress. At least two callers had reported that a teen was attempting to pry open the door of a Volkswagen with a screw driver. Both callers gave a good location and an exact description of both the car and the suspect.

When my officers arrived, they observed the car, observed the suspect, and watched as the suspect attempted to conceal the screwdriver in his pocket.

Upon detaining the suspect he made immediate pleas to anyone who would listen for someone to get his mamma. So someone did.

Mamma wasn't happy. Oh, she was fine with her son breaking into a car. She was not fine with us handcuffing him and placing him the back of one of our patrol vehicles. This prompted a call from the officers on the scene for a supervisor to respond.

When I arrived, one of my corporals was already there. Mamma was there raising a ruckus and getting more fired up by the minute. She's telling us what we can and can't do with her son and is threatening to sue us for excessive force (no force was ever used outside the application of the handcuffs).

As she's doing so, she moves over to the grass next to the sidewalk. While I'm getting briefed by the corporal, she is gradually growing more and more agitated and, with her foot, she's pushing sticks and other debris out away from where she is standing.

I tell my corporal, "Watch. She's going to pass out."

As he turns to look, Mamma makes a visual sweep of the area where she is standing, puts her hand to her forehead in a dramatic gesture, and crumples to the ground, being sure to do so in such a way as to make the landing as comfortable as possible.

Other people who have gathered start shouting, "Oh mamma, oh mamma!" and rush to her aid.

In a voice loud enough to carry, I tell my corporal, "Order a Code 2 ambulance with straps for a ride up to the Pavilion on a 5150 hold. This lady is obviously unable to care for her own safety."

Now, a 5150 is a psychiatric hold and the Pavilion is where all the 5150 holds go. This is common knowledge on the streets of my city, where people are familiar with our codes for being clear (Charlie) or having a warrant (Mary for matching information on file) or what some of the penal code sections are for robbery (211), burglary (459), and murder (187).

The lady promptly sits up. "I'm not crazy."

"No. But you're also not passed out on the lawn anymore which saves me the trouble of calling an ambulance for you."

Later she was writing down the names and badge numbers of all the officers for her "lawsuit". When she got to me, I courteously gave her my name, rank, and serial number and then asked for her name.

Mamma: "What do you want my name for?"

Me: "For the counter lawsuit."

Mamma: "You're going to sue me? For what?"

Me: "Slander, liable, and filing a false claim."

Mamma: "You can't do that."

Me: "Are you sure?"

Amazingly, her lawsuit never materialized.

VEGGIE BURGERS

I had assigned one of my sergeants and his squad to attend a community event in the west end of the city. Generally speaking, these events are opportunities for my officers to interact with the residents in a positive manner. A lot of times, the event organizers have food and family friendly beverages.

This particular sergeant doesn't like to eat food fixed by the community (he claims it's because he became sick one time from ill-prepared meat) and rather than be rude and simply tell them he doesn't trust their cooking, he had come up with a plan to avoid taking food while being polite. When offered a burger or hot dog, he would politely decline and say he was a vegetarian. This worked too, until this event.

At this community BBQ, he was offered a hamburger or a hotdog and gave his usual response. About ten minutes later, a man brings him what looks like a charred brick of meat between two buns. He says no thank you and repeats that he's a vegetarian. The man smiles, "It's a garden burger. No meat."

Turns out the only thing this sergeant hates more than eating food at a community event is eating vegetarian food at a community event.

BIKE PATROL

I'm certified to ride a bicycle for patrol duties. It's a lot of fun, once you get past the training class. During training, one of the exercises was to go down a very long flight of stairs at the local museum. On the day we attempted it, there was a large group of students waiting at the bottom of the stairs to get in. Each of the kids was maybe 6 or 7 years old. My first attempt was a flop...literally. I made it about half down and lost control of the bike. The rest of my decent was bumpy and rather painful as I fell down the stairs. The group of students were properly sympathetic and made all the appropriate noises that went along with such things. My second attempt was successful...the kids all clapped.

IS THAT A BIRD? IS THAT A PLANE? NO, IT'S BRICE.

While on patrol in the eastern part of the city, one of the officers, Brice, with me lost control of his bike while we were chasing a drug dealer and fell. Murphy's Law dictated that he fell in an appropriately brutal manner in front of as many witnesses as could be gathered at the time.

Several weeks later we were in the same area and were engaged in a foot pursuit of another suspect when Brice made a poor attempt to tackle our suspect and missed. For a moment, he looked like Superman in a black uniform. He was horizontal to the ground, about five feet up, with his arms stretched out in front of him. Even running, I could feel the impact as he hit the ground.

Not long after that I was on a call at that location and the complainant was explaining to me how she had already talked to one officer about this same incident. I asked which officer. "I don't know his name, but he's the white guy that falls all the time."

I didn't require a further description.

I THOUGHT IT WAS A GOOD IDEA

One Thursday night, the Chief and I were approached by two of the maintenance employees. Apparently, several days prior, one of the maintenance employees had parked in front of a business across the street from the Service Center. When he went out that evening, he found that one of his tires had been slashed. Today, he received a note on his car stating in summary that, vehicles that parked in front of the business were often damaged by big rigs that parked in the area and that the business was not responsible for any damage done. The note also encouraged the maintenance employee to find safer parking. He was showing the note to his colleague and discussing how his tires had been slashed. His colleague said that he parked in front of the business that day. When they went out to inspect his truck, they found that two of his tires had been slashed.

I'm not much of a traffic accident investigator, but I was pretty sure that while a big rig may cause some body damage to a vehicle it hit, I was also certain that a big rig did not slash tires.

The Chief and I decided that a special operation was in order where we would put out a couple of decoy vehicles and conduct a surveillance to see if anyone vandalized the cars. However, police cars don't make very good decoys, so we decided to use personal vehicles with the understanding that any tires slashed would be fixed or replaced by the PD. Not wanting to ask any of my officers to do something I wouldn't do myself, I volunteered my truck thinking that the worst that could happen was that I would get a new set of tires.

That Friday morning, bright and early, we have our decoy vehicles (my truck and one of my officer's cars) legally parked on the street in front of the business and we were set up at various points of observation. Now the waiting game begins.

Initially, the owner of the business had his two trucks parked in a parking lot right next to the business that is owned by the Sheriff's Office. At one point, one of the deputies had gone over and asked him to move them and he complied. Later he parked the truck he was driving back in the lot. They shut the gate on him forcing him to go seek their permission to open the gate and move his truck.

At around noon, he returned. Initially he was going to pull back into the county lot but with the gate closed, decided instead to parallel park in front of my truck. Now, there were at least 2 ½ car lengths in between my truck and the car in front of him. He backed into the space with his rear bumper about 6-10 feet from my front bumper, stopped for a few seconds, looked behind him and then hit the gas and rammed my truck. He then pulled forward back to where he had been.

Apparently (according to my officers), I was a little excited when I got on the radio and advised them that the owner of the company had just rammed my truck. The Chief contacted me on my cell phone and advised me to wait and see if he was going to do anything else. What? Like take a sledgehammer to my windows? Or, how about keying my door? That would be lovely.

Let me explain about my truck. I waited a long time to get this thing. I knew exactly what I wanted, what options, color, interior, everything. I hardly drive it and after a year and a half, it only has 14,000 miles on it and most of those were put on with a long trip to Colorado then to Texas, back to Colorado then back to California and two trips to Oregon. It had no damage on it at all. Of course, I was excited that this guy had just rammed it.

We waited. About 30 minutes later, the owner of the company comes back out to his truck, gets in, starts it up, and hits the gas backing up at a high rate of speed, once again hitting my truck. This time harder and I can clearly see the bumper get pushed back.

Last night, the loss of one or two tires that would be replaced that afternoon seemed like a good idea. Seeing my car get rammed not once, but twice, was almost more than I could handle. You think I was excited before.

Ok. No more waiting. I direct my officers to stop him as he takes off. They catch up to him and pull him over. When they detain him and tell him why, he says, "For what? Bumping a parked car?"

I arrive:

Me: "Have you ever been fishing?"

Owner: "Fishing?"

Me: "Yeah fishing. You know how you bait a hook to catch a fish? That truck was my bait and you were my fish. You've been caught. You're under arrest for felony vandalism and hit and run."

Owner: "For what? Bumping a parked car?"

Me: "Twice."

When he got down to the jail he started to hyperventilate. The jailer asked him what was wrong, and the business owner said he'd never been to jail before.

Jailer: "First time for everything."

Overtime for Special Operation: $325.00

Cost of Repairs to Decoy car: $695.95

Seeing the bastard who damaged your truck go to jail: Priceless

WHAT ARE THE CHANCES

What are the chances?

That in a city of 450,000 people where public housing residents make up less than 2% of the population that the vehicle that decides to run when my officers go to stop it would be tied to one of our properties?

In this case, extremely likely. Officers observed the vehicle traveling in the opposite direction from them at a high rate of speed and with no plates. When the officers swung around to pull it over, the vehicle's driver decided to make a run for it. He skidded across Telegraph Avenue and ran into a pole. As soon as I determined that the want on the vehicle was for traffic violations and a property hit and run only, I canceled any pursuit. Helpful citizens though led the officers to the car, now empty of its occupants. Upon tripping the VIN, the vehicle came back registered to one of our properties in the area, but without an apartment number attached to it. An astute officer asked to check it against the problem unit for that building and got a match. A few minutes, and a knock on the door later, the driver was in custody. He of course attempted to deny it, but the positive ID by the officers aside, he also had the keys to the vehicle still in his pocket. Score one for the home team.

WHERE ARE YOU?

One night on patrol with my rookie I asked him where we were at. He didn't know so I had him drive up to the next street sign and tell me. A while later, I had him stop the car in the middle of a block and asked him again, where we were. He didn't know so I made him get out of the car and walk up to the street sign and figure it out. Sometime after that I asked him again. This time when he didn't know I had him make a whole bunch of right turns and left turns until we ended up in the hills where there are long distances between street signs.

Me: "Stop the car. Where are we?"

Rookie: "I don't know."

Me: "Walk to the next street sign and look."

I spent the next 45 minutes catching up on his training manual. Guaranteed he didn't forget where he was again.

TICKET

I had one rookie that had a permanent case of cranial-rectal inversion. One night while we were on patrol he ran a stop sign.

Me: "Brent? What would you do if you observed a citizen run a sign right now?"

Brent: "Pull them over and give them a ticket."

Me: "Good. You just ran a stop sign back there. Next time you do that, I'm going to write a citation for it."

Brent: "What stop sign?"

Me: "Glad you were paying attention."

Not a few hours later, he runs another stop sign.

Me: "Brent, pull the car over and stop. You ran another stop sign."

I pulled out my ticket book, got his driver's license and wrote him a ticket. I let him hold on to his copy for the rest of the shift believing he would have to go to court on it. He didn't run stop signs after that.

ONLY IN MY CITY

One night there was another homicide. I say another because we had 90 other murders that year. This is not a crime problem in my opinion; it's an epidemic of considerable proportion.

Back to the homicide, a group of unknown assailants drive up in a car and open fire on a man standing on the side walk hitting him several times. The car then speeds off down the street. Two people who witness the shooting run to the "aid" of the victim.

Side Note: I said, "running to the aid of" with a little bit of trepidation, showing me for the jaded bastard that I am. A few years ago, there was a small Cessna type plane that crashed on 98th Avenue after a failed take off attempt (well sort of any way, it did take off it just didn't get very far). The pilot was in considerable pain and was trapped in his crushed plane. When the pilot saw people running towards him he was thinking to himself, "Thank goodness help is on the way." Those people left him with his pants and that only because his legs were pinned in the cockpit. People, to use the term loosely, stole his wallet, all his belongings, and the shirt (literally) off his back. In this case, there's no evidence to dispute that the two people that ran to help the victim had anything in mind except to do just that, they wanted to help a fellow human being who was hurt. To be fair though, this was a homicide and with the victim forever silent, who's left to argue with their account.

Back to the homicide, as the two people were rendering first aid, the suspect vehicle returns and shoots them for trying to help. Apparently, they wanted assurances that their target wasn't going to live through the night.

The suspect vehicle once again speeds off and runs head on into another car. The suspects bail out of the vehicle and take off running. The odd part is that the people in the car that was hit also all jump out and take off running.

When we arrive, we discover that both cars are stolen.

Now, what are the odds of something like this happening in your city? Two stolen vehicles running into each other in the middle of the night following, not one, but two drive-by shootings? In my city, those odds go up.

I love this city. I really do. It has history and culture and a lot of potential. It has great character even if that character is flawed. Only in my city can you hear the beautiful voices of a church choir raised in song praising the Lord on one side of you and a mother calling her children "dirty little f*ckers" and threatening to kick their good for nothing asses on the other.

KISS – KEEP IT SIMPLE STUPID

Sometimes the most obvious solutions are the best....

While coming back from a training exercise, one of my officers was flagged down on an injured animal call. Apparently, this dog had wondered out into the middle of the street and was hit by a truck. Unable to stop in time, the truck ended up dragging the poor animal approximately 30 feet. Four people had stopped to render assistance to the dog (my hat's off to the lady that works at plant shop down the street for staying the longest and for volunteering to find the dog a home if it survived). Two other officers who coming back from the training exercise stopped as well.

I ask for the status of the animal over the air and get back the response, "Its alive." Believing the worst and that we may have to dispatch the animal, I respond out there. I arrive to see a rather beat up looking dog lying on the roadway being petted by the lady from the plant shop. The dog is definitely injured, but doesn't appear so serious that it requires me to put him out of his misery (side note: This is something that I would do but would have a very hard time doing).

Now comes the hard part, what do we do with the dog. I have my dispatcher call to find out if Animal Control is on. No luck. Apparently, animals are only vicious or injured from 9 to 5. I have them call the emergency vet with no luck, they can take the dog but only if we can get him there. I consider using one of our cars, but we have these plastic, contoured seats that animals can't find purchase on and I was worried that the trip there would do him more harm than good. Plus, it's a big dog and according to the people there, attempts to move it earlier resulted in a very negative reaction on the part of the

20

dog (barking, growling, your typical "Hey look I'm hurting and I don't want you a-holes touching me" type of anti-social dog behavior). We need expert help here. I have the dispatcher call the County and the police departments in the four neighboring cities as well as the regional parks police. No one has as an Animal Control officer on duty.

By this time, all but the one lady has left. Almost 45 minutes have gone by and I'm no closer to getting this dog to the vet. The lady finally has to go as well. As soon as she's gone, the dog gets up and starts walking around. Still hurt but apparently not as seriously as we had first thought. I decide that the dog can be transported in the back of a patrol car.

I call up my corporal and tell him to rummage through the wood left after maintenance jobs and see if he can find a piece of plywood big enough to fit securely in the back of the patrol car and give the dog something besides an uneven plastic seat to lay on. I also ask him to bring the noose. As noted earlier, we had been advised that the dog objected to being moved and even though it was up and walking on its own, getting it in to the back of the patrol car was not going to be easy.

My corporal arrives. He has the noose. We get set up. The dog barks and growls and we give ground. We try again. The dog wins.... again. We step back, and we ponder. My youngest officer says, "Hey Sarge, why don't we see if it will just jump in the back of the car?" I'm a cynic. I don't believe it will work and say so, but we have nothing to lose so I tell him to try.

He goes over to the car and opens up the back door. "Come here doggy." The dog walks over to him and jumps right into the car.

Except for the little present the dog left for the officer in his squad car, the trip to vet was uneventful and by all indications at this point, the dog will be fine.

MILDLY AMUSING

There are certain advantages to being in an unmarked car. One of those is that people don't see you. Of course, that's a flaw too. Trying to go Code 3 in an unmarked police vehicle is a frightening experience. People don't see you.

One day I'm pulling into the apartment complex I affectionately call home. It's a large public housing complex where I traded a significantly reduced rate in rent (good for a guy who was paying his ex a fat alimony check at the time) in exchange for being a law enforcement presence in the neighborhood. At the four-way stop there at 85th Avenue and G Street there is a young man in a BMW doing donuts in the intersection. I watch as he completes the last of his rotations and attempts to take off down the street. Instead, he hits the curb and blows a tire. Having still not seen me, he pulls to the side of the road and gets out. He's staring accusingly at the flat tire as I pull up behind him and get out my car.

Me: "Hello sir."

Young Man: "Hello officer. I have a flat tire. Thanks for stopping though."

Me: "I see that, but that isn't the reason why I stopped. May I see your driver's license and registration please?"

Young Man: "For what? Having a flat tire? Man you guys are f*cked. I'm just a young black man with a broke down car and here you are jacking me. Police always harassing me. I go to school. I have a job. Shouldn't you be doing your job out arresting murders or something?"

(side note: This is one of my favorite things to hear. I would be more than happy to leave off whatever it is that I am doing at the moment to go arrest a murder. All anyone has to do is point one out and be willing to testify in court. I've never had any takers.)

Me: "Sir, this is a part of my job. I feel it's my duty to contact and identify those people who are engaged in activity that jeopardizes the public's safety. As an example, were I to see a person in a car, say a black BMW, doing donuts in the middle of the intersection and then have so little control over that car when they finish that they hit a curb and blow a tire, I might be inclined to stop them and ask them for their identification. Just as an example mind you."

Young Man: "Oh. You saw that."

Me: "Yes I did."

SUPER LADY KILLED TWICE AND CAN STILL TALK AND TALK AND TALK

My officers had responded to a drug call and after a foot pursuit had returned to the scene of the incident to make contact with the occupants of the apartment where the suspect had run from. As they were dealing with their business, I was carrying on a conversation with an older lady who lived in the front apartment. The lady was full of righteous anger and telling me in no uncertain terms how she felt about the drug problem and other issues that were going on at the property where she lived.

Lady: They make noise all night long and the police don't do anything about it. 2 or 3 in the morning and their banging the door and people running up and down the property. I've filed my reports and I'm going to a judge to do something about it.

I explained to the lady and told her that if people were running around late at night that she should continue to call the non-emergency number unless there was a situation where herself or others were in danger in which case she should dial 9-11 but, that I would attempt to help her with a more long-term solution.

Lady: Well, something needs to be done. There was the kid in an orange jacket that was walking around the side of my apartment with a rock (rock cocaine) in his hand. I had to yell at him and tell him to get out of here before I called the police. And these people around here with all their goings on just make it worse. They need to stop with all their intimidating and harassment and making noise at 2 or 3 in the morning. Some of them have some serious firepower out here such as I was liked to have passed out.

Me: Firepower? You mean….

Lady: I mean FIREPOWER, such as I was liked to have passed out. Shooting those needles and smoking that crack.

Me: Ma'am do you mean….

Lady: I mean FIREPOWER, such as I was liked to have passed out. I thought I was going to have to call an ambulance. I almost fell out right there and these people with their hollering and carrying on at 2 or 3 in the morning. Someone should do something about it. I have my reports.

Me: Ma'am, when you say firepower do you mean a….

Lady: I mean FIREPOWER, such as I was liked to have passed out. And them with their intimidating. I can't fight everyone you know but something has….

Me: …a gun?

Lady: I said FIREPOWER didn't I? You know I've been murdered twice since I've been here. Two times I've been killed. Did you know that?

Me: Up until this moment I would have thought it theoretically impossible.

Lady: I've been killed twice and I don't want there to be a third time.

Me: Ma'am, you have my word that you won't be killed a third time.

Lady: Thank you officer.

Me: You're welcome ma'am. Have a nice day.

I'M NOT A LAWYER

After arresting the drug dealer in a recent surveillance operation, the officers had relocated to a parking lot where they could complete the necessary paper work for booking the man into the City Jail. While attempting to obtain his basic information, the man refused to give his name. They called me over to see if I could talk to the guy.

Me: What's up sir? Why don't you want to give us your name?

Man: The officer read me my rights and said I had the right to remain silent. I'm remaining silent.

Me: Sir, you do have a constitutional right against making self-incriminating statements but that doesn't extend to obtaining identifying information like your name, address and date of birth. Unless there is something incriminating in your name, the right to remain silent doesn't apply.

Man: Your badge says Sergeant not lawyer.

I'll give the man credit for his powers of observation.

THE ATTEMPTED HOUDINI SHUFFLE

Recently during patrol, two of my officers were observing some narcotic activity in an area known as Cocoran Village when they spotted one subject engaged in some drug dealing. They contacted him, discovered he was on parole and searching him to ensure he was in compliance with the conditions of his parole, recovered enough marijuana to constitute possession for sales. The parolee was placed in the rear of a patrol car and while they were talking to him, he eluded that there was more drugs up inside one of the apartments.

By this time one of the supervisors had arrived on scene and he was watching the parolee while the two officers went to conduct a knock and talk at the apartment where the parolee said the drugs were at.

I'm not entirely clear on what happened next but as near as I can figure the parolee was complaining the handcuffs were riding on his bone and hurting him. The supervisor, being the nice guy that he is, decided to adjust the cuffs. As soon as one cuff was loose, the parolee attempted to escape. I say attempted because, much to the credit of the supervisor, he didn't succeed. The parolee, one hand now un-cuffed, made a mad dive for the window that had been opened for his comfort and was struggling to get out of it when the supervisor jumped in the car and grabbed the suspects legs.

Now, the two officers who had gone to do the knock and talk hadn't received an answer at the door and were returning back to their in-custody only to see him hanging half way out the car window. Relying on their finely tuned observational skills and utilizing their keen deductive reasoning, they quickly came to the conclusion that a person who had been arrested should not be hanging half way out of a patrol car window with the narrowness of the window being the only thing that separates them from a good felony arrest and an uncomfortable moment of explanation in my office.

They rushed over, pulled the guy the rest of the way out of the window and after a brief but futile struggle by the parolee, re-applied the handcuffs.

While they were pausing for a moment to catch their breath and to grumble about where the supervisor who was supposed to have been watching their in-custody had gone to, when they hear, "Ok guys, would you please let me out now?" They look and see the supervisor locked in the rear of the patrol car.

Apparently, while attempting to keep the parolee from escaping, the struggling suspect had pulled the supervisor all the way into the rear of the patrol car and the door had closed behind him. While it would normally be embarrassing to find yourself accidentally locked in the back of one of your own patrol vehicles, to his credit, when the supervisor had first jumped in to grab the parolee's legs he had smashed his elbow on the cage of the car effectively shattering it and he still managed to keep the suspect from escaping.

Imagine if the guy had managed to get away. I can almost see the looks on the faces of the two officers who left with the parolee seated in the back of the patrol car only to return to find their supervisor sitting there and their suspect gone. A trick like that would have done Houdini proud.

(As a side note, the supervisor was ok. He was off the streets for a bit while his bones healed but he was back to full duty in no time).

LITTERING

I'm driving behind a Chevy S-10 pick-up on the freeway when the driver tosses a cup out his window. The cup, apparently still containing soda, bounces off the hood of my car. The lid comes off and soda is splattered all over the hood, windshield and roof of my patrol car. Naturally, I'm a little annoyed and activate my lights intent on citing the litterbug. He pulls off the freeway and stops.

I approach him and make contact, before I can say anything he snaps out.

Driver: Transit Police!? Since when can the Transit Police do car stops on the freeway?

The transit authority has its own police department whose uniforms and vehicles were, at the time, similar to ours.

Me: I'm not with the Transit Police sir. I'm Officer Cotes and the reason I'm pulling you over is for littering on the freeway. I need to see your driver's license and registration please.

Driver: I didn't litter.

Me: Sir, you threw a cup out your window.

Driver: No, I didn't. You don't have anything better to do then harass innocent motorists? Shouldn't you be stopping a murderer or something?

Me: Sir, you did throw a cup out your window and I have the evidence to prove it.

Driver: What, you stop and pick up the cup off the freeway? Geez, you're unbelievable.

Me: Sir, would you please step out of your vehicle and take a look at my car.

With a little bit of grumbling and complaints that this will be like Rodney King, the man steps out and looks at my car. He quiets considerably and mumbles something under his breath.

Me: I'm sorry sir. I couldn't hear you.

Driver: I'm sorry. It slipped when I put my hand out the window.

Me: What slipped sir?

Driver, somewhat mollified: The cup.

Me: Just checking. If you'll have a seat back in your vehicle sir, I'll be with you in a moment, so you can sign the citation.

A WORD ON DISPATCHERS

One evening, I was working with my regular partner Tom in the east part of the city. Tom and I were very proactive and would often initiate stops as calls for service allowed. One Friday night, we couldn't turn a corner without on-viewing something. This caused us to stack (put back in the que or put on hold) calls that we had been dispatched to. After two of those, the dispatcher contacted our sergeant and told him to have us knock it off and just handle the calls. He met with us and passed along the information. We understood and had every intention of following that directive, but shortly after receiving our next call for service, we on-view a vehicle doing donuts right in front of us. We can't very well ignore it, so we ask for dispatch to stack the call while we do a car stop. You could almost feel her annoyance over the radio.

One citation, a crime report and a tow later we're back in service and ready for our next call...

Dispatch: 5A56 (5 Adam 56).

Us: 5A56.

Dispatch: Respond to a 415 family (family fight) at 6300 Hertz Street. Refused complainant advises that there are unknown people in an argument there.

Us: 5A56 copy but we're an East end unit and Hertz is on the opposite side of town in the north part of the city.

As we were both young back then, I'm sure the last was said with just a little cockiness thinking the dispatcher was confused about where Hertz was.

Dispatch: 5A56 I'm aware. Respond to 6300 Hertz Street on a 415 family.

Us: 5A56 10-4.

We respond to the north part of town and handle the call. When we go back in service (this time on the patrol channel for the west and north districts of the city), we're dispatched to some unknown address up in the hills on a possible alarm. When we clear that call (after many minutes looking at a map to figure out where it was) and go back in service on yet another channel for mid part of the city, we're dispatched back out to the east. We spent the rest of the shift going from one part of the city to the other.

At the end of our night, tired from being run all over town, our sergeant catches us in the locker room with one question.

Sergeant: Learn your lesson?

That we did. Never, ever piss off the dispatcher.

LOST IN TRANSLATION

One night I was dispatched up to the hospital to investigate a hit and run accident. Several of the five passengers who had been in the car that was hit had been injured, although none seriously. When I arrived at the hospital I discovered that none of the vehicle's occupants spoke English. When I found out that one of their friends had arrived at the hospital, who I was told could speak English and was willing to translate my questions into Cambodian, I had considered myself fortunate. At least until the interview began...

Me: Did they see the driver of the car that hit them?

The translator dutifully turned to the driver of the victim vehicle and asked him, presumably, the question I had stated. The driver spoke for several minutes and when he concluded, the translator turned back to me to relay the answer.

Translator: No.

Ok. Now I don't speak Cambodian, but I was certain that the language wasn't so complicated that it took several minutes to say no. Nonetheless, I accepted the answer and moved onto the next question.

Me: Were they able to get a look at the vehicle that hit them?

Once again the translator turned to the victim and asked my question (again, I assume that was what happened). The victim spoke at length to the translator and appeared very animated in the discussion and when the victim was done, the translator turned to me once again.

Translator: No.

Me: It took him that long just to say no?

Translator: Yes.

Me: Did he say anything more than just no?

Translator: Yes.

Me: What else did he say?

Translator: No.

Me: So all he said was no and it took him that long?

Translator: Yes.

Me: Are you sure that's all he said?

Translator: No.

Me (confused): You just said that all he said was no. Did he say something more than that or not?

Translator: No.

Me: Do you speak English?

Translator: No.

Ok, well that was helpful. On to plan B. Another person who allegedly spoke English had just arrived so I turned to them for help. This time we had a conversation first so that I was sure they spoke English. Good to go, I asked my first question again. After a few minutes discussion the translator relayed to me the following information:

Translator 2: No.

Me: What do you mean no? He said an awful lot just to say no. What else did he say?

Translator 2: He said no, he didn't see the man with the black hair and red shirt who was driving the red Ford car.

I'm sure I sighed, it was going to be a long, long night.

RAID

One Saturday morning I was working in my office when my dispatcher called down to advise me there was an irate lady on the phone demanding that we send someone out to deal with the ants that were in her house. On the weekends, nights and holidays, our police dispatch center will sometimes receive calls from the Housing Authority's emergency maintenance line. My dispatcher had told the lady that ants were not considered an emergency and that an emergency maintenance person would not be sent out unless she wanted to be charged the $85 for the visit. The lady felt that the charge was outrageous and instead wanted a police officer to come deal with the ants. My dispatcher told her that ants weren't a police matter. The lady went off and demanded to speak with a supervisor, hence the phone call to my office.

I picked up the line, identified myself and asked how I could help. The lady said that she had ants in her house and wanted something done about it. I suggested that she go down to the store and pick up a can of Raid. Snottily, the lady replied, "Can't you bring it to me?" I told her that ants weren't a police matter and that she could go to the store to pick up some bug spray. "I don't have a car and these ants aren't my problem, they're the Authority's problem and the Authority should do something about it." I told her that there was a corner market not half a block down from her apartment. "I can't walk. I'm elderly and this isn't my problem it's yours." At this point I started to feel a little frustrated.

Me: "Ma'am. I could request that a maintenance person be sent out, but because this isn't an emergency, you will be charged $85 for the visit."

Lady (yelling): "This is an emergency. I have ants in my house and I want something done about it. Can't you do anything?"

Me: "I did do something, I told you to go to the store and buy some Raid."

Lady (still yelling): "You bring it to me. It's your job."

I had moved beyond frustrated to the annoyed stage. "Actually, it isn't my job, but I'll tell you what, I'll be on my way over."

The lady yelled "good" and hung up the phone. I drove over to the west side of the city, stopped by the corner market and bought a can of bug spray. I then drove six houses down to our apartment complex and went and knocked on the door to the lady's unit.

The lady opened the door. Now I expected to see an elderly lady possibly with a cane. She couldn't, after all, walk a half a block down to the corner market and buy the can of bug spray herself. She was in her 50's. A long way from being "elderly" and the way she threw open the door, I didn't detect any infirmity that would have prevented her from making such a small trip. "About time you got here."

I handed her the bug spray. She looked like I was trying to give her a murder weapon covered in blood. "What am I supposed to do with this?"

"Here's a novel concept ma'am, let's read the directions on the can. Oh, it says here you point the nozzle at the infested area and press down on this button and the spray shoots out all on its own. Imagine that. Isn't technology something."

Lady (also annoyed): "I'm not spraying. This is your problem. You do it."

I bite back a sharp comment and walk into her kitchen and look around. Sure enough, there was a line of ants going from the window to the trashcan but that isn't what catches my attention. What catches my attention is the layer of grease on the windows and floors and the overflowing garbage spilling from the trashcan. I spray. Bugs die in droves. When I'm finished I hand the can over to the lady.

"Think you can handle this can by yourself?"

Lady: "Thank you officer. I don't know why they came in my place."

I have what I refer to as filters. Most days, the filters work like they are supposed to and sometimes, between a thought popping into my head and it reaching my mouth, it's been toned down sufficiently as to not be to blunt. Other days....

"I would imagine it has something to do with how filthy your house is. You have a layer of grime on the windows and floors and your trash is full and overflowing on to the ground. Try cleaning your house and maybe the ants won't come back. Enjoy the Raid compliments of the police department and have a nice day."

TOO EASY

So I'm sitting on a surveillance operation and it's going a little slow. A young man on a bicycle rides by taking a long swig out a Remy Martin bottle. In my city, there's a municipal code that prohibits having an open container of alcohol in public. As he gets closer to my car I step out to talk to him. Truthfully, I was bored and wasn't going to do anything more then tell him to pour it out.

Me: "Sir, let me talk to you for a moment."

Man: "F*ck you. I'm not doing anything."

He speeds up on his bicycle and rides by me before I get around the front of the car. I'm not overly broke up about it. Like I said, I was just bored and would have only told him to pour it out. As he continues to peddle away though he turns around in his seat and flips me off. Apparently, the combination of drinking, riding and making rude gestures was too much for him and he fails to pay attention to where he's going and promptly smacks into a street sign pole. I meander down to where he's laying on the ground groaning.

Me: "You alright?"

Man: "F*ck you."

I pick up the bottle of Remy Martin and pour it out. "I think you've had enough of this."

Sometimes, people make it too easy.

SENIOR CITIZEN VAULTS INTO
OLYMPIC HISTORY

We were working a special enforcement/enhanced patrol operation on the West End. One of my officers observed a vehicle run a stop sign and conducted a vehicle stop on it. It was a new PT Cruiser with tinted windows. Being nighttime, the tinted windows made it impossible to see into the cab of the car without increased lighting. As I was right down the street and had seen him pull the vehicle over, I rolled up to cover him on the stop.

By the time I pulled in behind the officer's car, he had turned on his spot light to illuminate the inside of the vehicle and was approaching on the driver's side. With the spot light, I could just make out the interior of the vehicle and could only see one person in the car…sitting on the passenger side.

The officer stopped at the driver's side window and, using his flashlight, looked into the car. He leaned a little closer and used his flashlight to sweep the inside of the PT Cruiser. Befuddled, he started to walk around to the passenger side of the car. I was also a little confused. While I didn't see a driver, I still assumed there was one as the vehicle had been moving when the officer pulled it over. I hadn't seen anyone run from the car but given the lighting at that time of night and the fact that I was a block away from where they stopped it was always possible that I missed that but as my officer was right behind the car when it pulled over and he never put anything out over the air (radio), I still expected a driver.

The officer contacted the passenger and after a few questions, asked him to step out of the vehicle and on to the sidewalk. The man had to have been in his 80's and age, not the chemically induced imbalance we so often see, was making it difficult for him to stand. With the elderly man out of the car, the officer checks the vehicle again. Closer now and not seeing anyone else in the car, I'm guessing that he's looking for the invisible driver. His check reveals nothing so he returns to the senior passenger. "Were you driving the car?" The man hems and haws for a second so the officer repeats his question a little more forcefully. Reluctantly the man answers yes and claims that he was going to get out of his car on the passenger side so that he was closer to the sidewalk.

Further checks reveal the older man has an outstanding warrant and no driver's license. A search of the vehicle uncovers 3 pieces of rock cocaine under the floor mat on the driver's side. When the search is all wrapped up, I look into the vehicle. There's a center console that, combined with the steering wheel, would make it difficult for anyone to smoothly move from the driver's side of the PT Cruiser to the passenger side and yet somehow, this old man did it and did it with enough speed that the officer didn't see him moving in the short amount of time it took for them to pull over and the officer to put the spot light on the car.

If rock cocaine can make an 80-year-old man nimble enough to vault a center console with a spryness that would make Paul Hamm blush with envy, I wonder why professional athletes even bother with steroids.

SPEEDING EXCUSES

I was driving eastbound in a fully marked patrol car when an older model Chevy goes roaring past me doing in excess of 20 mph over the posted speed limit. I pull in behind the car and activate my lights getting the Chevy to yield just a few blocks later. I approach the driver get his driver's license and registration and then tell him that I pulled him over for speeding and ask if he has any lawful reason why he was going as fast as he was.

Driver: Yes. I'm almost out of gas.

Me, slightly confused: How does almost being out of gas justify you're speeding?

Driver: I wanted to get home before I ran out.

I nod politely and go back to my car to write out the citation. When I'm done and return to the car I tell the driver that the way a car works, the faster you go, the more fuel you burn and therefore the faster you'll run out of gas.

Driver: Really?

Me: Really. Press hard, three copies.

SHOULD HAVE LISTENED

After making an on-view arrest I have my arrestee sitting hand-cuffed in the back of my car while I complete the paperwork necessary to book him in to the city jail. He's acting fidgety in the back of my car and I tell him to quit moving around so much.

Arrestee: Officer, I need to use the bathroom. Can you take the handcuffs off and just let me take a leak outside? I promise I won't run.

I get this same thing about every other arrest, so I mumble something about waiting till we get down to the jail feeling the guy must think I'm a rookie to fall for that line. He continues to fidget in the rear of my car so I tell him again to sit still.

Arrestee: Officer, I really need to take a leak. Can you hurry?

Me: I'm writing as fast as I can sir but I have to have this paper work finished before I can book you in to the jail.

As I'm finishing the short narrative on the bottom of the Consolidated Arrest Report, the guy is still squirming around in the back of the car. Half-heartedly, I tell him to sit still again and this time, he stops moving around so much allowing me to complete the paperwork. As I start to drive towards the jail I ask if he's ready to go.

Arrestee: No rush.

Feeling a little smug that he's finally giving me credit for not being stupid enough to un-handcuff him and let him out of the car so he can take a leak I sarcastically ask, "I thought you had to go to the bathroom?"

Arrestee: I already did.

Damn!

A good hosing out and a bottle of bleach later at least I'm no longer making faces when I get into the car.

FREUDIAN SLIP

We're working a special operation in the west side of the City when the communication center receives a 911 hang-up call from an apartment in one of the major developments located in the same area as our operation so they forward it to my team. When 911 is dialed, the computer system records the telephone number and address where the call originated from. When no one stays on the line, officers are dispatched out to the location to ensure that everything is fine.

When the officers knocked on the door of the residence they were greeted by a young man. A few questions established that he wasn't a resident and was allegedly the cousin of the legal tenant although her name escaped him. Having a responsibility to make sure that everything was all right at the unit, officers did a quick look around and then identified the young man.

According to the young man, he had been trying to call a person in the Sacramento area. Instead of dialing 1-916-***-**** he dialed 9-116-***-****. The telephone system only picked up the fact that he dialed 911 and automatically connected him to dispatch center. As soon as they picked up, he hung up which prompted our response to the apartment.

Upon running a quick check on the young man it was discovered that he was on probation for drug sales with a four-way search clause. Invoking the search clause to ensure that he was in compliance with the terms of his probation, the officer conducting the search discovered 18 individually packaged 1"x1" sacks of marijuana. Oops.

Called the police on himself. Must have been a Freudian slip.

PACKING HEAT

On my way into work one morning I noticed a Ford Explorer parked along the street near my apartment. The vehicle was perched precariously upon some cinder blocks and was missing some of its tires. Suspecting it might by abandoned or stolen, I requested that dispatch run the plate out. Unfortunately, our computer system was down, and I wasn't able to get a return before getting to work. Once there though, the computer system was back up and upon running the plate, dispatch advised me that it was a stolen vehicle. I had them stack the call for an officer and went about my daily work.

About noon I received a call from one of my neighbors who advised me that a man and a woman were stripping the car. I immediately responded and when I arrived, I did in fact find two people attempting to remove the remaining tires from the Explorer. Both were placed under arrest.

During the search of the man incident to arrest, I asked if he had any weapons. He told me that he had a gun in his right pocket. Upon searching his pocket, I found only a 1" metal, toy gun. "This?" I asked, slightly confused. "Yes." he replied sincerely. Curious, I asked why he had told me he had a gun and why he was carrying the little toy.

"In this city, you have to be strapped, even if it's only symbolic."

Check. I guess it's better the symbolic packing of a gun then the reality.

ID PLEASE

I've had some interesting forms of identification presented to me before. Naturally I've had the typical check cashing cards, probation papers, bills, etc. but two of my favorites had to be a CD cover and the girl with her name and date of birth tattooed on her stomach.

Me: Ma'am, do you have some ID? A driver's license or similar?

Lady: Can you read?

Of course my first thought was to respond with something like, "No. I actually got this job based on my good looks and charming personality and my uncanny ability to put up with bullshit responses."

Me (a little flat): Yes.

She lifts up her shirt and points to her stomach where, tattooed neatly, is her name and date of birth. How cute.

On a car stop I asked a gentleman for his driver's license and registration.

Man: Uh, I don't have a driver's license.

Me: You have a California ID?

Man: Not on me.

Me: You have anything with your name on it?

Man: Uh, yeah. I have this.

He hands me a CD cover with his face on it titled, "Gansta Rap with DZ Kidd" (that wasn't the actual name but it was along those lines).

Me: Wow! You're DZ Kidd?

Man (a little smug): Yeah. You've heard of me?

Me: No. Just seemed like an appropriate response. A CD cover isn't considered acceptable ID and I doubt your parents named you DZ. You have anything else?

Man: No. Just that. It's me. Really. Just look at it.

I look at the CD cover again. Not that it will change anything but what the heck. I flip it over and look at the list of songs. Number one on the program, "Cop Killa."

Me: Sir, for your safety and mine, could you please step out of the vehicle and keep your hands where I can see them.

END OF THE DAY... NOT

It's the end of a long day and I'm on my way home. I'm talking with my friend and generally thinking life is good.

I'm sitting in the left turn lane, waiting for traffic going the opposite direction to clear enough so that the vehicle in front of me can go. Apparently, he wasn't as patient. Suddenly he guns the engine and whips into a turn...right in front of another vehicle.

These are moments that seem to slow down. Your mind is calculating the rate of turn of vehicle 1 with the speed of vehicle 2 and even before they hit, you know the inevitable outcome.

CRASH! Broadside collision. The vehicles stop for a moment then casually pull off to the side of the road. Although I want to go home, and I do have my friend on the phone, it's a no go. Can't ignore it as much as I want to. I make a hasty goodbye and pull in behind the two cars.

Good news. No one is hurt and both cars are drivable. I help to facilitate the exchange of information. As I return to my car, one of my officers pulls up to check on me.

We're sitting there talking for just a moment when a transit bus screeches to a halt right in front of us and a frantic bus driver jumps off flapping her arms wildly.

Houston, we have a problem. Oh, did I mention I was on my way home.

We dutifully exit our vehicles and approach the breathless bus driver. She explains that a lady had a seizure on the bus and hit her head on one of the seat bars.

For those of you who have suffered, or seen head wounds, they're nasty. The smallest cut can pump what seems to be volumes of blood.

We get on the bus. The lady is coming out of her seizure but is now realizing she's hurt. She's panicking a little but telling her what occurred seems to have a calming effect, at least on the lady. The bus driver on the other hand has had too much.

From behind me I hear a loud thump. It's a distinctive sound. Anyone who has ever stood in a military style formation for too long and had someone lock up their knees knows that sound. The sound of a human body hitting the floor...hard.

I turn and gaze at the prone bus driver who has passed out cold. My officer's guess was that the blood got to her. My guess was that the plastic thingy that holds the six pack together snapped. Differences of opinion aside, we order our second ambulance.

As I turn to assist in reviving the bus driver my attention is caught by the man sitting right behind the driver's seat. He's in his late 40's, early 50's and is cradling a backpack to his chest.

Now generally this wouldn't be enough to catch and hold my eye, but I'm a trained observer. I also notice the fact that he is cursing under his breath and doing that rocking back and forth thing that you generally associate with someone on the edge.

As I bend down to check on the bus driver whose eyes are starting to now flutter open, I ask the man if he's ok.

Side bar: Isn't that a rhetorical question? The man is hugging a back pack, rocking back and forth and muttering angrily. I'm no Freud but taking a shot in the dark, I would say he's a long way from being ok.

He glares at me. "NO! I'm not ok. Do I look ok? I just want to get to my class. I'm late for my class. Can't you just take them off the bus so I CAN GET TO MY CLASS!"

Alrighty then. There are a few things that run through my head at this point. First and foremost of those is, even if I wanted to remove the two ladies from the bus, one of them is the bus driver so who the heck is going to drive?

I divert myself away from that question, seeing ways in which it might be misinterpreted. Tomorrow's headlines, "Psycho drives off with bus full of people after cop asks stupid question."

"No sir, not at the moment anyway. Your bus driver is just coming to and see the lady with the gushing head wound. I think my partner and I intend to keep her right there until the ambulance arrives."

You can't blame me for trying to explain reasonably. The guy leaps out of his seat. "I DON'T GIVE A F*CK. I NEED TO GET TO MY CLASS. I'LL BE LATE."

There is a part of my brain that shuts down when confronted with situations like this. I like to think of it as a filter. On a good day, the filter works as advertised and I say nothing to aggravate a situation, other days....well, if you've been annoyed by me in the past, raise your hand.

"Sir, you have two options here. You can wait for the bus driver to feel a little better and the lady to be taken off by the paramedics or you can walk. Notice that one of your choices was not to yell at the police officer. There's a reason for that. Right now, I don't have the time or the patience to deal with it and I'm more likely to stuff you in the back of a patrol car than I am to listen to you. So, what is it going to be?"

The guy blinks at me and quietly sits back down. He's decided to wait, how noble. Within a few moments the bus driver is up and walking around, feeling much better. The paramedics and fire department are on scene taking care of those who need it. And a spare bus is pulling up so that this one can be taken in and washed out.

My officer will handle it from here. As I start to exit the bus, the guy tells me, "You should go to that class too."

"What kind of class is it?"

"Anger management."

Touché.

It's time to go home.

MISSING IN ACTION

I was assigned to work patrol on the westside of town. While cruising around one of the large public housing developments in that area, I heard a possible shooting call go out over the patrol channel not far from my location. At the time, I was driving a white, marked police vehicle.

As I make the corner and see the location where the shooting was supposed to have taken place, I see only one black and white patrol car there (I didn't see the unmarked car in front of that, but that isn't really important). I decide to cover the officer and pull in behind his vehicle.

I turn off my engine, remove my keys and place them in a holder on my belt and exit my car. As I shut the door, I don't lock it. I seldom did back then. If I had to leave in a hurry, it saved a few seconds not to have to unlock the car door.

I meet with the officer and the sergeant who was driving the unmarked (which now I see). He explains the call. They had a report of a shooting, but they can't find any victim. No blood trail, spent shell casings or anything else to indicate that a shooting had taken place, but he wants to check behind a store just in case the victim was there. He asks if I can assist. As assisting is the reason I stopped in the first place, I don't have a problem with this.

As we start down the side of the store and begin to make the corner to the rear of the building I hear the roar of an engine and the screeching of tires. I glance back and see a white patrol car race by. I step back out, so I can have a clear view of the street and see the vehicle tear wildly around a corner and head the wrong way down a one-way street.

My first thought was that I didn't hear any of my units (those driving white police vehicles) hit off here and I didn't hear any calls on our channel that would necessitate such a speedy response. But, it looked like one of our patrol cars so mentally I start marking off the locations of all my fellow units. Joe and Art were on a call in the east, Tom was at the City Jail dropping off a prisoner, one officer was at the station and another was on his lunch break. That accounted for all our units. While there are other agencies in the area that also drive white patrol cars, I can't figure out why any of them would be in this area particularly.

My stomach starts to sink. If it isn't one of the other units, and it's unlikely that it was a different agency, then that leaves only one white patrol car in the vicinity...mine.

I step out onto the street and see that my car is in fact, gone.

Now all of this takes but a moment. I immediately get on the radio.

Me: 16L2 (my call sign).

Dispatch: 16L2 go ahead.

Me: 16L2, my vehicle is 10851 (said Ten Eight Fifty-one, stolen car) and last seen heading westbound going the wrong way on 8th Street.

Sergeant: 16L73, repeat that last traffic.

Dispatch: I believe he said his vehicle is 10851. 16L2 confirm?

Me: 16L2 affirm. My vehicle is 10851. If it helps, I have my keys.

The officers I was assisting step up next to me and ask what happened. I can hear their radio clearly, "Units in the area. A citizen reports that a Transit Authority police car just ran into a tree in the 900 block of Union Street. Can I get a Code 3 (lights and siren) response to check on injuries?"

I mentioned that there are other police departments with white cars. I'm no geography wiz but I think the likelihood of a Transit Authority police car smacking into a tree just about two blocks from where I'm standing is a little more than coincidental. Grudgingly, I tell the municipal officer that it most likely isn't a Transit Authority vehicle but mine. Dutifully (and I swear with a smirk on his face) he advises his dispatch that it most likely a Housing Authority police car wedged against that tree and that it was just stolen from the 900 block of Nelson Parkway.

The municipal officers jump in their cars and roar off to the scene of the accident leaving me standing on the corner pondering my misfortune. Eventually, my sergeant comes and gets me, and we drive over to the accident scene.

It's somewhat disheartening to see your formerly well running police car with the front end smashed against a tree. The person who stole it is sitting in the back of a squad car. When the air bag deployed it knocked her for a loop. She attempted to run but only made it about 3 feet before collapsing to the ground unconscious.

Here's what happened. This lady, drunk on alcohol and high on crack (she was very honest about her condition), had heard that you didn't need a key to start a police car. She was walking down the street and saw these two police cruisers just sitting there. She tried mine and found that the door was unlocked and decided to give the theory a try. Lo and behold, the car started when she turned the ignition. The theory isn't correct unless you have a screwed-up ignition, which apparently my car did have. Now, she's sitting behind the wheel of a running police car and decided it wasn't good to leave it there, so she concludes that she must take it back to the station (or so she says). The car got a little away from her and bam, that tree jumped right in front of her.

We now have a totaled patrol car.

The next day I get to go visit the Lieutenant. There are no rules or regulations that say you have to lock your car, or at least there wasn't, there was by the time I got to the Lieutenant's office. So, there is nothing to discipline me on, but I was admonished not to ever do that again.

Point taken. I lock my car every time I step out of it and heaven help any trainee I have who leaves his door unlocked.

Years later, I was attending a class being put on by one of the area academies and the instructor was talking about patrol tactics and mentioned that you should always take your keys with you and lock your car door. As an example, he told us about this poor Transit Authority officer whose car was stolen by a drunk lady and rammed into a tree.

Instructor: "That's what happens when you leave your car keys in the ignition and don't lock your doors."

Me: "Excuse me sir, but that officer actually did have his keys. The ignition was screwed up."

Instructor: "Oh, you know the officer?"

Me: (face turning a little red) "You could say that."

I only felt a little guilty for letting the Transit Authority take the heat for my stolen car.

TOUCHED BY GOD

My partner and I had been dispatched to a call regarding a lady who was possibly in need of psychiatric evaluation. Her daughter felt that she was no longer stable and wanted her committed.

We arrive on scene and meet with the complainant. While my partner talks to the daughter in the kitchen, I talk with the lady in the living room. We are the only four people in the apartment. I ask her the standard questions. Do you know what day it is? What month? Time of day? Do you feel like hurting yourself or others?

She answers each question, and as I talk to her, she seems in perfect control of herself. Confused as to why the daughter thought her mother was losing it, I explain why we are there to the lady. She seems shocked. "I'm not insane. Ask anyone. You can ask Bob or Donna or John. They'll tell you."

I think this is a good idea. After all, the daughter could have an ulterior motive here (ok, admittedly I'm somewhat jaded). I tell the lady I would like to talk with these other people and ask where I might find them.

She looks peeved. "They are sitting right here. Go ahead Bob, tell the officer I am perfectly sane."

I did mention we were the only four people in apartment right? The daughter, the mom, my partner, and me. Ok then.

I tell the lady to have a seat and that we're going to have some nice paramedics come and take her to see a doctor. She sits down in a chair and I advise my partner we'll be ordering the ambulance now.

When the paramedics arrive, they come in and start talking to the lady. They ask her the same questions I did earlier and get the same responses. One of the paramedics asks me why she's being committed. I tell him to trust me and that I wouldn't fill out the paper if it wasn't necessary. The paramedic shrugs his shoulders but goes along with it.

Paramedic: Ma'am, if you'll stand up we'll walk down to the ambulance and you can get on the gurney then.

Lady: No. The nice officer told me to sit here and here is where I'm going to sit.

Paramedic: I know Ma'am, but it's ok to get up now.

Lady: No. I was told to sit here. I'm not moving.

Me: Ma'am. I'm the officer who told you to sit there. Its ok to get up now. These are the nice men I told you about who are going to take you to see the doctor.

Lady: No. The officer said to sit here and I'm not moving.

We have a dilemma. We have an old lady who is refusing to move and we don't want to force her to get up because it looks bad to have 3 grown men forcing a little old lady up out of a chair.

As we are sitting there pondering the problem, the lady jumps straight up out of the chair and raises her hands above her head and yells, "GLORY BE TO GOD IN HEAVEN."

At the time, the clip to my pager had broken and so I kept it in the left, breast pocket of my uniform shirt. For tactical reasons, it was set on vibrate (bad form to be sneaking up to a suspect and have your pager go "BEEP, BEEP, BEEP").

At the exact moment when the lady jumped up and yelled about God, my pager goes off. Did I mention it was in my left pocket, you know, the one right above your heart. For a moment, I thought I had been touched by the holy spirit. I came unglued and almost fell out right there. When I realized what had happened, I started laughing and was in fact laughing so hard, that I couldn't make anything more than a wheezing noise.

The paramedics now had the lady up but where concerned about my welfare. It was a while before I could tell them what had occurred.

We all got a good laugh out of that.

58

UNLUCKIEST MAN ALIVE

While I was still on field training, my FTO (Field Training Officer) and I were dispatched to an unwanted guest call. As we pull up to the scene, I see a middle-aged man and an older woman arguing in the doorway of an apartment. We exit our car and start walking up. As we do so, the man attempts to force his way into the apartment. The lady pushes him back and reaches behind her. When her hand comes out, she's holding a heavy frying pan, which she then uses to crack the man upside the head with, knocking him cleanly on his ass.

While the frying pan knocked him for a loop, it didn't knock him out and he jumps up and starts to force his way back in. He sees us though, and immediately starts running. Being the rookie, I immediately start chasing him.

He runs west bound through the complex and out on to Unica Street. A car traveling north on Unica Street doesn't have enough time to stop as the man runs out in front of it. BAM! The car strikes the man causing him to be thrown up on the hood of the car. Doing what any reasonable driver would do, the driver slams on the brakes causing the man to roll off the hood and smack right on the ground.

Does this stop the man? No. He gets up and keeps running and being the rookie, I keep chasing him.

He runs north up Unica street and then cuts into the yards. I hear a lot of screaming and cursing. As I run down the side of a house where the man went, I see the cause of the screaming. The top of the fence he is trying to climb over is lined with razor wire. He succeeds in getting over the fence just as I get to it.

I'm smarter than the average bear, so I stop at the fence. Razor wire and I don't get along. So here we are. I'm on one side of the fence and the man is on the other. He's been hit in the head by a frying pan, ran over by a car and sliced and diced by razor wire. I try and tell him that I'm not interested in taking him to jail, but a hospital might be in order. He tells me with extremely colorful language to go away. As we are standing there debating our different points of view, I hear a growl and look down just in time to see a Rottweiler lunge for the man, grabbing his leg in its large jaws, and shaking hard.

The man's string of curse words is cut off by the large dog that now has a hold of his leg, and turns into screaming. Somehow, the man gets away from the dog and manages to escape over another fence.

By this time the block is locked down by other officers and a tight perimeter has been set. We begin doing a yard by yard search for this guy. I'm about to give up and call it a day when I glance up and see just one bloody shoe hanging over the edge of a shed. I'm on the other side of a fence from the guy but I call out to him

He responds with his now familiar string of cursing. I tell him that he's surrounded and that he is to come down so that he can be taken to a hospital. He complies and jumps off the building...and decides to run.

Unfortunately, the way he chooses to run is guarded by several other officers, one of whom used to be a defensive lineman for a professional football team. Just as the man nears the end of the driveway he is running out of, he is greeted by 250 lbs of police officer and unceremoniously taken to the ground, where several other officer pile on to help control the guy and handcuff him.

Let me recap this man's day. He was hit in the head with a frying pan, ran over by a car, sliced up by razor wire, mauled by a Rottweiler, and tackled by a former professional football player. You see why I call him the unluckiest man alive?

Turns out the lady who hit him with the frying pan was his mother. He was a crack addict and needed money and she wasn't going to give him any. While in this case, crack didn't kill, it sure hurt like hell.

BUT, BUT DAD....?

It must have been a really busy night because my partner and I were in an old Ford LTD, unmarked with a magnetic red light that had nothing fancier than an on/off switch. It was the only car left in the fleet and with good reason. While these Fords had big engines and were light weight, they ran for crap and stalled if you took a turn too quick. This will be important later.

We were on patrol in the east. We had handled a few calls but for the most part it was a dull Friday night. As we came to a halt at a four way stop sign, a moped with two riders blows through the stop sign with no lights on. Neither of the riders was wearing a helmet, and both of them had to be in excess of 200 lbs. I would have said it went whizzing through the stop sign, but with over 400 lbs. on it, the moped was really groaning rather than whizzing.

We activate our red light and the cute little siren that goes with it and pull in behind the moped. Do they stop? Of course not. We are now in pursuit.

Again, I point out that there was over 400 lbs. on this moped and so it wasn't really what you would call a high-speed pursuit. In fact, I think our top speed never exceeded 35 mph. To make our job simpler, the guy driving the moped just kept going in circles around several blocks. We'd make the corner, our vehicle would stall, we'd start it up and never lose our position as the primary in the pursuit. We were going so slow I started keeping a running tally of all the vehicle code violations the driver was committing.

Once the driver slowed down and the passenger jumped off. My partner, who was driving, slowed down and I jumped out of the car and handcuffed the passenger. When everyone made the block again, my partner stopped so I could put our detainee in the back of the car and we continued our pursuit.

This continued until we had a tight perimeter with nowhere for the guy on the moped to go. He ditches the bike and starts running through the yards. I exit the car and start chasing him.

He hops a fence and is about to go over another one when he sees squad cars pulling up right where he wants to go. He can't go back knowing he's being chased, so he goes for what's behind door number three. Actually it wasn't a door, but a window. He busts out the window of a house and crawls through.

I'm too late getting over the fence to stop him, so I hop the fence he was going to just in time to see an old man run out of the house yelling that someone just broke in and for someone to call the police. Imagine his surprise to find about 10 cops already standing on his neatly manicured lawn.

We charge into the house and into the living room. In a chair is an old lady with a death grip on the arms of said chair. Laying on the couch sweating profusely in nothing but his underwear looking for all the world like he belonged there was our suspect.

The old man points and says, "That's him. That's the man that broke in our house."

Our suspect affects a wounded look, one full of shock and disbelief and replies, "But, but....dad?"

ROOKIES

While training a new officer we are going south on Cole Street and he then turns east on 8th Street. The only problem with 8th Street is that it runs one-way and not in the direction my rookie is going.

Me: "Brent, notice anything wrong with the way those cars are parked." Referring to vehicles on our "side" of the road.

Brent: "Yeah. They're parked facing the wrong direction."

Me: "All of them?"

Brent: "Yeah. All of them."

Me: "What are you going to do about it?"

Brent: "Cite them."

Me: "Ok. Stop the car."

He dutifully cited about 7 or 8 cars before he saw the one-way sign. After collecting all the tickets he had written, he got back in the car.

Me: "Shall we go now."

Brent: "Uhhhh, yes."

LEPRECHAUN

One of my officers, Jose, is infamous for his inability to speak a lick of Spanish, despite growing up in a household with parents who spoke fluent Spanish. He often gets clowned about it. One day he and Connor an Irish guy, are in the locker room and Rob is giving him a hard time.

Connor: "Jose, the only Spanish you know is yo quiero taco bell."

Jose: "Yeah, like you speak Irish."

Connor: "Next time you pull over a leprechaun, let me know."

OF MICE AND MEN

We were serving a search warrant on 74th Avenue. When we arrived on scene my officers lined up perfectly, coolly competent in their approach. The knock and notice was done, and when there wasn't an answer, the breacher moved up and popped the door in one shot. Entry was made. Two people were taken into custody inside the apartment, drugs were recovered as well as two guns including an assault rifle.

It was as perfect an execution of a search warrant as I had ever seen my officers accomplish. As their sergeant, I was proud.

While we were conducting the search of the rest of the apartment I was standing in the living room while two of the officers were searching a storage space underneath the stairs.

I heard a yell followed by an "ohhhh shit" and the two officers came tearing out of the storage area at a full run and headed out the door. One of them kept repeating over and over, in a high-pitched voice, "Mouse, mouse, mouse..."

I went to investigate what was in the storage area that had scared my officers half to death only to discover a small little brown mouse. They refused to come back in till it was removed.

I had to laugh. Here are some of the finest police officers I have ever had the pleasure of working with. They had just calmly made entry into a dope house and recovered guns without ever batting an eyelash only to be sent scurrying for the hills by a mouse.

CREEPING

I like to do what I call creeping. Basically, I think the standard law enforcement tactic of driving up on a group of drug dealers and jumping out of your car is over used and often results in a foot pursuit that we, as cops, too often lose. I'm wearing a full uniform that includes about 30 extra pounds of gear, plus boots, racing a kid in a t-shirt, tennis shoes, and jeans. So, I adapted my Marine Corps training in stealth tactics to my current profession and came up with creeping. Sneaking around in the dark and using cover and concealment to hide your whereabouts.

Generally, in order to use creeping to its fullest advantage, you need to scout an area first. Right after going back to night shift patrol, I was working 75th Avenue and had discovered a hole in a fence that led from 64th Avenue to the back of an apartment complex and from there you could sneak along the side of the building, and out on to 75th.

My first scouting expedition though was almost a flop. I went the wrong way around the building and was spotted by one of the dealers. I heard him yell, "Five-0" (signal that cops are in the area) and everyone took off running.

Free to look around now I used it to my advantage and found an old car sitting in the yard of the apartment complex. The car was surrounded by about knee-high grass. I hunkered down by the front of the car where the shadow of the vehicle combined with the high grass effectively made me invisible. Now came the waiting game.

Patience is a virtue. Within 20 minutes two of the drug dealers returned. I could see them walking up the street asking each other where I was.

Drug Dealer 1: Where is he?

Drug Dealer 2: I don't know man. I think he's gone.

Drug Dealer 1: He's not gone. He's still here somewhere.

Drug Dealer 2: No man, he's gone.

Drug Dealer 1: Are you sure?

Drug Dealer 2: Yeah.

Drug Dealer 1: Ok.

DD1 then proceeded to retrieve his stash of drugs from its current hiding place and then walk across the street right to where I was hiding. I lost sight of him for a minute, but I could hear the grass rustling to the side and knew he was close. A second later I see his hand reach down through the grass not 6 inches from my head and put his drugs by the front tire of the car where I was hiding. I say he was hiding his drugs but, what I mean was that he thought he was hiding his drugs.

He then stands up and moves out on to the side walk where he waits for customers. I casually reach out and take his stash. He didn't have to wait long for a customer. Someone pulls up. The drug dealer steps off the side walk and behind the fence. He turns back toward the street to make sure it's all clear. I use this opportunity to stand up in full view right behind him.

The look on his face when he turned back around was classic. His lips were moving but no sound was coming out.

"Gotcha!"

LITMUS TEST

I was riding with Mark. While technically my trainee, Mark and I had been reserve police officers together and so it wasn't quite the same as having an officer who was fresh out of the academy.

Mark on-viewed a possible hand-to-hand drug transaction in the 3000 block of College Street so we conducted a vehicle stop. Before we could get up to our suspect though he swallowed whatever drugs he had purchased. Nonetheless, he looked like he was under the influence of narcotics so we were going to take him for that. He was read his Miranda rights after being handcuffed, and placed in the back of the patrol car.

While there are always abject symptoms of drug use, dilated or restricted pupils, sweaty or clammy skin, speech, vertical or horizontal nystagmus (a rapid involuntary oscillation of the eyeballs), etc., it's always easier for them to tell you what they are on.

Mark started running the standard tests and asking the guy questions. The guy wasn't budging though and insisted that he wasn't on anything. I was standing there listening when Mark gives it a last ditch effort.

Mark: "Man, I can tell you're on something. Your eyes are all screwed up, you're sweating and you're talking too fast. What'd you take?"

Man: "I didn't take anything officer. You got it all wrong. I'm just nervous."

Mark: "Look. You can tell me what you're high on or I can have my partner there administer an in the field drug test. If it turns out you're lying you'll spend a lot longer in jail."

Man: "Look, I haven't taken anything. I swear."

Mark: "Ok. Hey Wayne, would you get one of those field test kits for drug use and test this guy?"

I always tell my rookies that their greatest tool as a police officer is their mind and the best skill they can develop is their ability to bullshit. However, when bullshitting, it's always nice to have a plan and even better to include your partner in on the plan. We had no field test kits for drug use and I'm not even sure that such a thing exists for use by police officers. Mark was bluffing. I know this and go to the trunk of the car to act like I'm getting something out.

Mark: "Now my partner is getting the test kit. One more chance to tell me the truth."

Man: "I'm telling you officer, I didn't use anything."

Bluff called.

Mark: "Ok then. We'll just have to test you."

Mark walks to the rear of the car and tells me that he thought the bluff would work. Another rule I always tell my rookies is to have a back up plan and if possible, to have a back up plan to the back up plan. We didn't have a plan to begin with so I'm initially thinking we're screwed on this little interrogation. Mark suggests that we just grab something that looks like it would be a drug test kit and use that. Another bluff.

I quickly search the trunk of the car and my eyes light upon a citation that Mark had made a mistake on earlier in the day. At the end of the citation is a little perforated tab that holds the three copies of the citation together. One side is white and the other is pink. I remember the litmus paper from biology class and an idea forms.

I take the little tab and walk over to the back door of the patrol car.

Me: "This is the litmus drug test. It works real simple. You'll notice that it is currently white." I hold up the white side to demonstrate my

69

point. "I'm going to place it on your forehead and if it turns pink you've been using drugs. Understand?"

Man: "Ok. I'll tell you. I smoked some weed this morning but that's all I swear."

Me: "I'm not a doctor but I've been doing this long enough to know that weed doesn't cause the symptoms you have so what else did you take?"

Man: "Nothing I swear."

I push the ticket tab to the guy's forehead and as I pull it off I flip it over so that it shows the pink side, which I display so the man can see it.

Me: "Pink."

Man: "Ok, ok. I was shooting up heroine last night and it left me feeling down this morning so I smoked a rock. The rock had me too hyper so I came over here to buy some weed. Can we just go to jail now?"

AUTHORITY

I arrest a guy on an outstanding warrant and as he's sitting in the back of my car he proceeds to tell me that I don't have the authority to arrest him on a warrant.

Me: "You know sir, you're absolutely right. I'll just have to make something up then."

Man: "Hey! You can't do that."

Me: "According to you I don't have the authority to arrest you on your warrant either but that didn't stop me."

Silence.

DO YOU KNOW WHO I AM PART 1

I stop a car for running a stop sign and approach the driver to give my standard car stop spiel.

Me: "Hi. I'm Officer Cotes and the reason I pulled you over is that you ran that stop sign at 38th Avenue and Santa Marie. May I see you license and registration please?"

The man hands me his license and registration and I return to my car to write him the citation. When I get back to his car I hand him the citation and ask him to sign.

Man: "You're giving me a ticket?"

Me: "Yes sir."

Man: "Don't you know who I am?"

Me: "It says here on your driver's license that you're Robert Smith."

Man: "You mean you don't know who I am?"

Me: "Well sir, if you're not Robert Smith then we have a problem because I have his license with your picture on it and if Robert Smith isn't your name, that generally results in something more than just a citation."

The man signs the citation angrily and hands it back to me.

Man: "God you're stupid."

Me: "Thank you sir. Have a nice day."

DO YOU KNOW WHO I AM PART 2

I stop a car for speeding on San Leonardo Blvd and approach the driver.

Me: "Hi. I'm Sergeant Cotes and the reason I pulled you over was you were speeding. May I see your license and registration please?"

The man hands me his license and registration.

Man: "Do you know who I am?"

Me, looking at the license: "Why yes sir I do. You're Roy Robertson."

Man: "Good. Does that name mean anything to you?"

Me: "That you're a powerful Hollywood movie executive and I'm going to be famous?"

Man: "No."

Me: "Then I'll be right back with your citation."

AMUSED ME

While patrolling the west I see a truck driver in a semi stop at 14th Avenue and Monroe to pick up what appears at an initial glance to be a woman. The problem with 14th and Monroe is that it's the local hang out for all the transvestite prostitutes.

I follow the semi and pull it over after it fails to signal a turn. I explain to the truck driver, a rather large, bearded man, why I pulled him over and that I had seen him pick up the "lady". They both give me a story about how the "lady" and the truck driver's sister were friends and that he was just giving "her" a ride home. I tell them I'm aware the area is a high prostitution area and I was checking to be sure. I obtain both of their ID's and run a warrant check. When I'm done and both come back clear I hand them back their ID's.

Me: "Here you go Mr. Jones (truck driver)."

Jones: "Thank you."

Me: "And here you go Mr. Edwards (passenger)."

Jones: "Mr. Edwards?" Turning a nice shade of red going on purple.

Me: "Yes sir. I figured that given Mr. Edwards and your sister were such good friends that you knew he was a man. I'll just leave you two to go about your business."

Mr. Edwards: "Oh god no officer! This man was going to pay me $20 for a blow job and you can take me to jail but don't leave me alone with him."

TOM AND DERICK

Tom and Derick were consistently partners and they had a penchant for getting into things. Tom was 6'03" and couldn't have weighed more than 150 lbs. and Derick was 6'01" and topped 300.

WHY CLIMB WHEN YOU CAN RIDE

Tom, Derick, and I got dispatched to a drug call in Westside Gardens, one of the large public housing developments in the city. As we pull up into the parking lot of the complex, we have several subjects run from us. They exhibited amazing athletic skill by quickly scaling a 10-foot iron fence and disappearing into the complex. Tom takes off running after them. When he gets to the fence he quickly assesses the situation and decides that the easiest way to climb the fence is to go over at the gate which has a cross-section that makes climbing it easier. Just as Tom reaches the top and has slung one leg over so that he is now on the straddling the top of the gate, Derick arrives...and pushes on the gate. It swings slowly open with a surprised Tom riding it.

He said he'd kill us if we ever told anyone.

TUG OF WAR

I heard Tom and Derick hit out in the 2200 block of 48th Avenue. One of hotter drug spots and knowing them, I start rolling that way. Within a minute they are in a foot pursuit.

I increase my response to Code 3 and pull up in time to see a suspect half way across the top of a high fence. On one side, holding onto the suspects legs, his own feet braced against the fence to give himself leverage, and pulling on the suspect for all he is worth, was

Tom. On the opposite side of the fence, holding onto the suspects arms and pulling for all he was worth was Derick.

Both of them had gone opposite directions when this poor guy started running. Tom in direct pursuit and Derick attempting to head the guy off. When the guy hit the fence, Tom was right behind him and grabbed a hold of his legs to pull him back down. It was working too until Derick saw the guy on top of the fence and thought he was trying to back off of it to get away from him and so grabbed his arms and started trying to stop him by pulling him his way. Both officers think this guy is resisting their attempts to get him off the fence and can't figure out why he is so blasted strong.

SCARY MOMENTS

We were conducting an impromptu surveillance of a property on Hillside. Tom, decked out in all black, snuck over some fences and through some back yards to get out onto the street and into a position where he could see the property. He found some bushes along the sidewalk that afforded him a good view of the activity while providing him great concealment.

As Tom is watching a guy walks up the sidewalk and stops right in front of where Tom is hiding. After glancing up and down the street, the guy turns to face Tom, still not knowing he's there, and unzips his pants to take a leak.

Tom, horrified that he's about to get pissed on, stands straight up, yelling, "Put it back. Put it back."

The guy thinks he's getting robbed and starts crying.

I'm not sure who was more afraid, Tom, or the poor guy who just needed to take a leak.

THERE'S SOMETHING ABOUT SHERRIE

One extremely rainy night at about 1:30 am, I was dispatched to the lobby of the Police Department to pick up a senior resident who had been robbed in a neighboring city and didn't have keys to get back into her apartment. I was sent to see if I could assist her in making entry.

When I arrived, I met with the desk officer who directed me to Sherrie. Sherrie was standing by the doors opposite where I came in and holding her shoes in her hands. As I started to walk over to her, the desk officer made a motion with his hands that left me with the faint impression Sherrie maybe a few fries short of a happy meal.

When I walked up to her, I introduced myself.

Me: "Hi. I'm Officer Cotes with the Police Department and I'll be taking you over to your apartment and, hopefully, letting you in."

Sherrie: "No, that's ok. I'll wait for security."

Me: "Ma'am, there is no security, just police. If you'll come with me though I'll let you in."

Sherrie: "No, that's ok. I'll just wait for security."

Me (with a sigh): "Ma'am, I'm Officer Cotes with the Security people. I'll let you into your apartment."

Sherrie: "Oh, ok. Thank you."

As we started heading for the door I told her that it was raining pretty hard outside and that she should probably put on her shoes so her feet didn't get wet.

Sherrie: "No that's ok. I'll leave them off so my feet don't get wet."

Me: "Ma'am, if you don't want your feet to get wet, I'd put your shoes on."

Sherrie: "No, that's ok. I want them to stay dry."

Ok then. When we got to the car we had a brief discussion over why she couldn't sit up front and then proceeded on our way. She immediately started telling me about her bird.

Sherrie: "Now, when we go in, we have to be very quiet so we don't wake up my bird. If we wake him up, he's a canary and he'll sing all night long and I'll never be able to get some sleep so we need to be very quiet. Did I tell you that I buried my canary in a field of lilies? But if we wake him up he will sing all night long so we have to be very quiet."

Yes, she did in fact say she buried her canary in a field of lilies.

Right in the middle of her commentary about her bird and waking him up, she stops and yells at the top of her lungs, "AND NOW IT'S TIME FOR THE ENTERTAINMENT!" And then starts singing, "I have bubble gum on my shoe. I have bubble gum on my shoe."

My sergeant at the time was anal about getting off exactly at the end of shift and 2 am was fast approaching. I hear him call me on the radio and ask how long I'll be. I tell him that I may be awhile because this one is looking like a green sheet (green is the color of the form you fill out for a psychiatric detention). Naturally he asked why. I just held the radio up and keyed the microphone.

Sergeant (sounding resigned): 10-4.

THERE'S SOMETHING ABOUT SHERRIE PART TWO

My trainee and I were dispatched to one of the senior complexes regarding a lady on the 6th floor screaming and banging on doors. The complainant wanted her to be quiet.

When we arrived and exited the elevator on to the 6th Floor we saw Sherrie lying prone on the floor of the hallway. Her eyes were glassy and wide open, and she was covered with blood from her head down to her waist. My first thought was that she had been attacked and was screaming for help and banging on doors and now she was dead.

I immediately called for an ambulance and sent my trainee down to the lobby to guide them in. While he was taking care of that, I started calling Sherrie's name and approaching her cautiously (cautiously so that I didn't disturb something that might later be of evidentiary value in a criminal case). I repeated her name several times without getting a response.

When I got close enough, and still calling her name, I reach down to shake her a little. Again, I didn't get a response. I was convinced she was dead. As I went to check her pulse though her head turned slowly towards me and she looked me straight in the eye...

Sherrie: "Did I tell you my gopher has a motor home?"

I'm came unglued and must have jumped about 10 feet back.

What had happened was, Sherrie had become drunk and fell down hitting her head (hence all the blood) and was banging on door to get a band-aid.

There is definitely something about Sherrie.

BODY SNATCHERS

One night Erv and I were dispatched to investigate a burglary. When we arrived, we met with our complainant, Mr. McCully. Mr. McCully told us that someone had broke into his apartment and stolen a radio. He was the perfect complainant. He had the make and model of the radio, how much he paid for it, and most importantly, the serial number.

While Erv obtained all the information, I checked around the apartment looking for a point of entry. I checked the front door and didn't see any signs that it was forced. The lock was still intact and there weren't pry marks on the door to indicate it had been jimmied.

I checked all the windows. None of them were broken and they were all locked. The same with the patio door. I was baffled.

I returned to Mr. McCully and asked him a few questions about the condition of his apartment when he arrived home. He told me that all the windows were closed and locked and the front door was locked when he got home. I asked if anyone had a key to his apartment and he said no. Now I was really confused. How does a perp get into a fully locked apartment and not leave a trace.

Me: "Mr. McCully, I'm a little confused here. I've checked your entire apartment and I don't see any signs of forced entry. According to you, all the windows and doors were locked when you got home and no one besides you has a key. Any idea how they may have got in?"

Mr. McCully: "Oh, didn't I tell you? They're body snatchers."

Check. Erv and I had to make a hasty departure before our professional demeanor broke.

DUMB COP STORIES

Even police officers have their moments.

FIRE

16L6: "Code 33 (emergency traffic). We have a major fire in Logpine (one of our larger apartment complexes). Send me additional units. I'll be switching over for the fire department."

I started rolling that way Code 3 (lights and siren). When I arrive at where 16L6 is at, I see two socks on fire on a cloth line. I return to my patrol car and get the fire extinguisher and put them out.

Me: "16L7, you can cancel fire."

I HAVE A BOO-BOO

16L6: "11-99! 11-99! (officer needs immediate assistance)"

Dispatch: "Units we'll be Code 33 (emergency traffic). 16L6 what's your location?"

16L6: "67th Avenue and 14th Street. I'm hurt and bleeding badly. I need a Code 3 ambulance."

Dispatch: "Units to cover? I'll be ordering Code 3 medical."

Me: "16L7 responding Code 3."

Sergeant: "16L77 responding Code 3."

The Sergeant and I arrive at the same time and see 16L6 hunched over. A handcuffed suspect is laying on the ground next him.

Sergeant: "What's wrong? Are you ok?"

16L6: "No. I'm hurt. I need an ambulance."

Sergeant: "Where are you hurt?"

16L6 then holds out his hand and shows us a tiny cut on his finger. Apparently when he was handcuffing the guy on the ground he got a little skin from his finger caught in the cuffs when he closed them and it cut his finger.

Sergeant: "16L77, you can cancel the Code 3 medical. A band-aid will suffice."

RIGHT THERE

After a surveillance operation, I called the units in to pick up our main dealer.

Me over the radio from my surveillance spot: "You all are going after the subject wearing the red t-shirt and white jeans. He's easy to spot. He'll be standing on the east side of the street. Go ahead and come in."

The units swoop in and our suspect starts walking off down the street.

Me: "16L6 that's the subject right there to your left. Grab him."

16L6: "Where? I don't see him."

Me: "He's right there to your left about 2 feet from your car."

16L6: "Which one?"

Me, sounding peeved no doubt: "He's the only one and he's wearing a bright red t-shirt."

Fortunately, someone else snatched him up.

NOBODY LIKES ME PART 1

116L6: "16L6, is there another unit that can respond to contact a warrant suspect I'm spotting."

Me: "16L7, I'm right around the corner, I'll be there in a second."

16L6: "Ok. Hurry, he's walking up on me."

Me: "16L7 10-4. Be right there."

16L6: "He's right by my car, he's right by my car. Hurry."

Dispatch: "16L6 do you want me to hold the air?"

16L6: "16L6 negative. I just need another unit to contact him."

A few seconds later…

16L6: "Cancel my cover. My suspect went into the store."

Now I'm confused. 16L6 is a police officer with all the powers invested therein and for the life of me I can't figure out why he didn't stop this guy so when I pull up, I ask him.

16L6: "He doesn't like me."

WTF!??

NOBODY LIKES ME PART 2

Moses and I were on a 5150 (psych detention) combative and had finally got her strapped to the gurney and were standing by while the paramedics loaded her up in the ambulance. 16L6 walks up behind us.

16L6: "See that guy over there."

I look over and see one of our main dealers standing not far away. "Yeah."

16L6: "I admonished him for trespassing yesterday. He's good to go on a 602 (trespassing) arrest."

Me: "Ok."

16L6: "Someone should go arrest him."

Me: "You're the one that admonished him. If you want him arrested, go ahead, I'll cover you."

16L6: "No, no. That's ok. He doesn't like me. I just thought you all should know."

NOBODY LIKES ME PART 3

16L6: "16L6, can I get a cover unit for an uncooperative?"

Me: "16L7, I'm nearby. I'll take the cover."

I pull up and see 16L6 arguing with an older lady trying to convince her to give him her identification. She's refusing. As soon as I walk up though she pulls out her ID and hands it to me.

Lady: "You can ID me Officer Cotes, you can take me to jail, you can do whatever you want, but I will not talk to that man a moment longer. I don't like him." She points at 16L6.

DOH!

While working a prostitution sting I was partnered up with Hodge. While completing an arrest report, Hodge looks at me and asks me how to spell "his".

Me: You mean, H-I-S, his?

Hodge: Yes. How do you spell it?

DOH! PART TWO

Derick was working with a particularly flustered trainee who kept asking him how to spell words while he was completing the arrest report. They were sitting in the sally port at the jail and the suspect was still in the back of the car. After asking Derick how to spell a particularly easy word, the suspect responds, "Dude. You need hooked on phonics."

DOH! PART THREE

Tom was riding with a trainee and on-viewed a hand to hand drug sale and quickly snatched up the dealer, handcuffed him and turned him over to his trainee to watch while Tom took off in foot pursuit of the buyer. Tom caught the buyer about a block away and upon searching him, found a piece of rock cocaine. Feeling pretty proud that he's got two felony pops (one for possession and one for sales) he starts to get on the radio and have his trainee transport the other suspect over to his location when he sees his trainee make the block. When the car pulls up next to him, Tom sees the dealer isn't in the back of the car and asks his trainee where the dealer is.

Trainee: "I asked him to stay where he was, and he promised he would."

Of course the guy was gone, with Tom's extra cuffs. Just goes to show you that you can't trust the word of a drug dealer.

BUSY

Troy and I were on patrol and had a long day and were feeling pretty lazy when we got dispatched to a report of a man who was drunk and had passed out on the lawn of an office building. When we pulled up I hit the air horn to rouse him.

Once he was more or less conscious and still not having left my car, I called him over to my window. "Hey boss, you're drunk and need to go downtown to sober up. You cool with that?"

Suspect1: "Ok."

Me: "Excellent. Empty out your pockets on the hood of my car."

When he had done so and there was nothing in them of note, I handed him a pair of cuffs and had him put them on and get in the back seat. From there we relocated to the parking lot of the McDonald's to wait for a wagon to transport.

While in the parking lot we see a guy on a bike. He's staring at us as he rides by and suddenly falls over.

Troy: "Hey man, you ok?", yelling out our car window.

Suspect2: "Yeah. I'm just really drunk."

Troy: "Ok. You need to go down town and sober up."

Suspect2: "Ok."

Me: "Alright man, empty out your pockets on the hood of the car and put these on when you're done." I handed the guy my other set of cuffs. Once everything was out of his pockets and put back, he cuffed himself and got in the back of the car with our first subject.

We continued to wait for the wagon when we were approached by a man who worked for the auto shop right next to the McDonald's. He told me that this guy he knew had a warrant and that the guy wanted to know how he could get it cleared up. I told him to send the guy over to us and we'd help him.

Within a few minutes, the guy with the warrant comes up to my window.

Suspect 3: "Yeah, I have a warrant and want to know how I clear it up."

I get his name and date of birth and run him. Sure enough, he comes back with a warrant that he can't be cited out on.

Me: "The only way you can take care of this warrant is to go see a judge tomorrow and the only way to see the judge tomorrow is for me to arrest you on the warrant. What do you want to do?"

Suspect3: "I want to take care of the warrant."

Me: "Ok. Empty your pockets on the hood of the car."

While this guy finished with his pockets I got a pair of cuffs from Troy and had the guy put them on and pack himself into the back of the car. We now had three suspects in-custody and had never left our vehicle.

Within a few minutes, the wagon arrived.

Wagon Officer: "I thought you guys only had one for transport."

Troy deadpans: "We did, but we've been busy."

Side Note: This was really bad officer safety. Never confuse good luck with good tactics.

FAIR PLAY

We were swooping in to arrest a drug dealer one night. As soon as we pulled up the dealer took off running and a foot pursuit ensued. I chased him down 26th Avenue and then east onto Logan Street before he cut up into the yards and jumped a 4-foot-high fence. I was right behind him. It was pitch black in the yard we were in, but I could see a shadow running away from me. I drew my gun and chased it across the yard yelling, "Freeze! Police!" When the shadow stopped at the back fence I finally managed to get out my flashlight and illuminated the area only to see that what I chased across the yard was a large German Shepard and he wasn't happy. Turn about being fair play, he chased me the opposite direction.

GOOD SCARES

My partner and I got dispatched to a burglary and upon our arrival we met with the reporting person, a young man who was house sitting for friends of his parents. The front door was kicked open and the evidence that someone had rifled the place looking for loot was all over the living room. My partner and I draw our guns and starting sweeping the house just in case the suspects were still there. In a bedroom we got to a sliding door that appeared to be a closet. I opened the door while my partner covered me. What was actually behind the door wasn't a closet but a bathroom and in the bathroom was a big black lab who came bouncing out happy as can be scaring the crap out of both my partner and me. For the rest of our search he chased the beams of our flashlights.

My partner and I were dispatched to the burglary of a law office. We were sweeping the offices for suspects and my partner opened a closet door causing a mop to fall on him. While it scared the daylights out of both of us, he screamed like (forgive me ladies) a woman. The rest of our search was conducted with me trying in vain to suppress my laughter while he kept mumbling, "Shut up. Don't tell anybody."

FINGERS

I went out on a walking stop on 3 subjects I suspected were involved in drug sales at 32nd Street and MLK. As I was exiting my car, I called the three over to me. I then locked my door and shut it. Only problem was I forgot to move my hand and managed to get four fingers shut in the door. To make matters worse, it was my gun hand. I was dead in the water and even though it hurt like hell, I played it off. I calmly asked a few questions, thanked them for their time and as soon as they walked away, quickly unlocked my door and removed my fingers.

AT HOME PATROL

For a time, I was a resident police officer in the deep east part of my city. For those not familiar with resident police officers, in exchange for a discounted rent payment, I lived in one of the public housing complexes. In this case, a large development with over 100 units. I had long been opposed to mandatory residency requirements for police officers (something my city tried to do for a bit) but in truth, after living in this community for almost five years, I can see why cities think it is important. It was a rewarding experience and people stop seeing you as a police officer and start seeing you as a person who shares their struggles of living in a high-crime neighborhood.

Several times a day, when I'm home, I take Dexter (my dog) for a walk and I use the opportunity for patrolling the property.

One day I'm out walking around (in civilian clothes) and over by the park I see a car parked. Standing across the street on the side walk is a man. Getting out of the front passenger side of the car is a woman and sitting in the back seat is another man.

As I watch, the woman goes around to the driver's side back door and opens it up. I can see into the car and notice that the man in the back seat has his pants pulled down around his ankles. The woman then starts clearing the garbage out of the back seat and throwing it on the ground.

Guy standing outside of the car + Guy in the back seat with pants down + woman + this particular block = Prostitution. Standard equation.

I approach the woman.

Me: "Hi. I'm Sergeant Cotes. I'm the resident police officer here. You need to pick up the trash and take your business elsewhere."

Woman to guy standing across the street: "He says he's the police and we need to go."

Me: "No. You need to pick up the trash and then go."

The guy walks over and asks what the woman said.

Woman: "He says he's the police and that we need to pick up our trash and go."

Man: "He ain't the f*cking police."

Me: "Sir, I either am who I say I am or I'm just some really crazy white guy. Either way, I'd go."

Man: "Let's get out of here."

Wise choice. Even in civilian clothes, I'm still a cop.

TOO EARLY IN THE DAY

One morning I'm out walking Dexter, and as I walk by the park I see two people sitting at one of the tables. Between the two of them is a small black bag. On the table is a bottle cap stuffed with cotton.

Oh joy, heroin addicts (the black bag is what's called a hype kit, usually contains a surgical band of some sort for tying off on the arm and exposing the veins, needles and a cooker which generally takes the form of a bottle cap or a spoon. The cotton if for straining the heroin once it's been cooked...don't ask, I have no idea why).

I walk up.

Me: "Mind if I contribute something to the party?"

Woman: "Sure."

Man: "What you got?"

Me as I sit down and place my badge on the table: "A word of advice."

Man: "F*ck."

Me, smiling: "This is my park and my home, and I don't want drugs anywhere near my little corner of the world. No matter how nice you two may be, it still sets a bad example for the kids and I want the kids living here to be free of those influences. Do we understand one another?"

Man: We were just leaving sir.

Another wise choice.

SLEIGHT OF HAND

One day I get home and I'm in a hurry. I have to be at a community meeting for my complex but I need to walk Dexter first, so I grab him and, still in uniform, head out along the railroad tracks. As I'm walking out the gate to the park parking lot, I see a black pick-up with 3 people in it driving towards me and pull into a parking stall.

I walk over to the rail road tracks while the dog does his thing and watch the truck. As I'm watching, I see the male passenger of the truck pull a crack pipe to his lips and burn it.

People playing baseball and soccer in the park and these morons decide to smoke a rock right in front of God and everyone. I tie Dexter to the fence and approach the truck (I always love that "oh shit" look people get on their faces when they see me).

The passenger rolls down his window. "Can I help you officer?"

Me: "Yes. Give me the crack pipe."

Passenger: "What crack pipe?"

Me: "Look boss, I've been doing this for quite a few years. Save the innocent, don't know what you're talking about lines for a rookie. I don't have the time. Give me the crack pipe."

Passenger: "What pipe?"

Me sighing: "Open your hand."

This had to be the worst slight of hand I've ever seen. It wasn't even remotely smooth as he switches the pipe from one hand to the other.

Passenger: "See, I don't have anything." He said, opening up the now empty hand.

Me: "You're other hand sir."

Ok, the second worst slight of hand as he drops the pipe on the floor board of the truck.

Passenger: "See, I'm clean."

Me: "Step out of the truck."

Passenger: "Why?"

Me opening the door of the truck and pointing at the pipe: "That's why. I tried to tell you not to play with me and now we have to do this the hard way. Step out of the truck."

The passenger complies. I handcuff him, search him and have him have a seat on the sidewalk while I recover the crack pipe and a small piece of rock cocaine from the floor board of the truck. I then pull the woman in the middle out and search her quickly for officer safety and have her have a seat. I then pull out the driver.

Remember Dexter tied to the fence? When I first embarked on this little adventure there was no one around. People in the park, but no one close enough to bother me. In between pulling the driver out of the truck and searching and handcuffing him, ten kids sprung up around Dexter like weeds. I have no idea where they came from. One minute it was clear, the next they were all there.

Me: "Hey. You all leave the dog alone ok."

Random Kid 1: "Its ok Mr. Policeman. We'll watch Dexter for you (the kids in my neighborhood can't remember my name for anything. They will either call me Mr. Policeman or OG which stands for original gangster meaning I've been around for a while)."

Me: "Kids, I'm busy. Just leave him be."

At this point I can no longer see my dog. He is being mobbed by kids. One little girl is trying to untie his leash from the fence.

Random Kid 2: "We'll take him for his walk Mr. Policeman."

Me: "Please leave him alone guys."

Random Kid 3: "Does he bite? Ouch!"

Random Kid 4: "What kind of dog is he?"

Random Kid 1: "I want to walk him."

Random Kid 2: "No. I'm walking him."

Me: "KIDS! STEP AWAY FROM THE DOG!"

Random Kid 6: "Its ok Mr. Policeman, we'll protect him."

Dexter: "YELP!"

Ok, I now have a dilemma. Dexter is a little dog, only about 12 lbs., and he is surrounded by little kids. Not always the best formula for a worry-free day. I turn to my suspect.

Me: "Sir. I have a problem. I can't deal with you and rescue my dog at the same time. You've seen me unsuccessfully try and get the kids to go away. I'm thinking I'll have better luck making you go away. You want to leave?"

Passenger: "Yes sir."

Me: "I thought so. Problem is, you're under arrest for possession of narcotics. However, if I were to accidentally drop this piece of rock on the ground next to your foot and you were to accidentally step on it then I wouldn't have any evidence and therefore I wouldn't be able to arrest you. You follow me?"

Passenger: "Yes sir."

I then drop the rock cocaine on the ground next to his foot. He continues to just stare at me not moving.

Me: "Look. I told you that if I didn't have evidence I couldn't arrest you which means you wouldn't go to jail. I "accidentally" dropped the rock on the ground. Now, you "accidentally" step on it."

Still a blank stare.

Me sounding flustered as Dexter yelps again: "Boss, step on the rock."

Realization finally dawns on him and he steps on the rock and after some prompting, grinds it into uselessness (this was probably a worse punishment then going to jail).

Me: "Look at that. No more rock. Now, when I accidentally drop this pipe on the ground you accidentally step on it as well. Got it?"

Passenger: "Yes sir."

I drop the pipe and get immediate results. My friendly neighborhood drug user has figured out how the game is played. I quickly un-handcuff the two men and the woman and tell them to leave never to return on penalty of their freedom. They are quick to comply. I then wade through the mass of kids and rescue my poor dog.

Consequently, I was still on time for my community meeting.

CHAOS BUBBLE

I'm sitting in my apartment minding my own business and watching a movie on TV and the next thing I know I have people in the parking lot blasting music and yelling and cussing at the top of their lungs.

My work offers a resident officer program. Move into a public housing complex and you get a discounted rent. So, I move into one of the largest housing developments in the city. For the most part it's cool but every now and then I have a night like tonight.

Being me I get up to investigate what the heck is going on. I step outside and there are two car loads of people in the parking lot behind my apartment. They're guzzling booze like its water, have the car doors open and the stereos cranked and they're dancing but not just in the parking lot. They are dancing on my unmarked patrol car.

Two women are bumping and grinding on the roof then one of them has the gall to yell out to me, "What's up bitch?"

Me: Let's get one thing straight real fast, I'm not anyone's bitch, but unless you get off my car with a quickness you will be. Her name is going to be Bertha and she's going to be 600 pounds of pure malice, and your cell mate. Understand? Smart people crawl off my car.

Then my favorite part, drunk ass dude decides he wants to be a hero and tell me "F**k the police."

Me: Boss, you come to my house, have people dancing on my car and then you want to disrespect me. Have you taken leave of your senses? Have you consumed so much alcohol that it has overridden your common sense, short circuited your brain housing group and rendered you dumber than a blade of grass?

Obviously, my dander is up. I'm on my off time, at home, trying to watch a little TV, in the peace and quiet of my tiny apartment.

Admittedly I often say things that get me into trouble. It's both a curse and a blessing. People always know that I speak my mind and so there isn't any guess work involved but it does occasionally cause my Chief grief when he hears from an offended citizen how I spoke just a little too much of it.

Apparently this person didn't like my pointed questions and thought he would express his displeasure grabbing a stick and waving it about like he was King Arthur with Excalibur. Who was to know that pepper spray has a range of over 15', and that not only do I carry a set of handcuffs off duty, but I'm also the departmental weaponless defense instructor and teach officers how to use said handcuffs...effectively. Then this skinny little twig of a girl wants to get up in my face like I haven't had my patience tested enough for one night. Do you really want to join your friend on the ground crying and wondering how to make the burning stop? Thought not. I really don't like arresting women any way. I'm funny like that but won't let a person's gender stop me from doing my job or protecting myself.

And after all that, I missed my movie. That really pissed me off.

WHAT ARE THE CHANCES?

That in one evening, in the complex where I live as the resident officer, there would be a burglary, a man setting things on fire, a family fight where the son went sidewise on mom, a drug recovery and a medical call all inside of an hour?

Generally, not even a consideration but on that Tuesday, the cards must of have been stacked against my officers. While on my way to have dinner with my fiancée' and my future in-laws, I received a call from one of my neighbors advising me that her house had been burglarized. I'm out of town so I call dispatch and ask if they have an officer available to head over to that unit for the investigation and report. I'm in luck, an officer is in the green (clear) and dispatch sends them out. While en route, they get a priority call that a man is setting things on fire in front of another unit in the same complex as the burglary. They break and head to that. While on scene at the fire starter incident, one of the neighbors runs out of their apartment and yells at the officers that "Larry" has gone crazy and is beating up his mom. They break from the fire thing and go investigate that. Larry is gone, but while attempting to decipher what happened, the Sergeant on scene is approached by a lady who promptly holds out her hand and declares she just bought these... in her palm are two pieces of suspected rock cocaine. That doesn't happen very often. Well actually, to my knowledge, it's never happened but hey, I had only been around for 15 years at that point.

The officers finally make it over to the burglary call. While canvassing the neighbors for any possible witnesses, the officer knocks on a door and when it opens she's greeted by an hysterical occupant,

"Oh thank god you're here, he's about to die and has gone into a diabetic coma!"

When it rains it pours.

KIDS

Yesterday, when I got off from work, I was out walking my dog. Some new kids that recently moved into the neighborhood see him and start asking questions. Things like, "Is that your dog?", "How big will he be when he grows up?", etc.

Kid1: Mr. Policeman, is that your dog?

Me: Yes it is.

Kid2: What kind of dog is he?

Me: He's a Norwegian Mouse Hound (this is an on-going joke that started with my mom, he's in fact just a mutt).

Kid1: How big will he be when he grows up?

Me: He is all grown up. He's as big as he's going to get.

Kid3: Really?

Me: Yep.

Kid2: Ain't much of a dog then.

Me: He's all the dog I need.

Kid4: What's his name?

Me: Dexter.

Kid2: Does he bite?

Me: He hasn't bit anyone yet.

Kid4: I think I'll call him Cocoa.

Me: But his name is Dexter.

Kid4: I don't like that name. I like Cocoa.

Me: But Cocoa isn't his name.

Kid4 (reaching down to pet Dexter): Hi Cocoa.

Me: What's your name?

Kid4: Meisha.

Me: I think I'll call you Joe.

Kid4: Joe? That's a boy's name.

Me: I know, but I think I'll call you Joe.

Kid4: But that's not my name.

Me: And Cocoa isn't Dexter's name either. He likes to be called Dexter just like you like to be called Meisha.

Kid4: But I don't like Dexter so I'll call him Cocoa.

Me: Then I will call you Joe.

Kid4, looking very sad: You don't like my name Mr. Policeman?

Me: Awww....no, no honey, I like your name just fine.

Kid4, smiling: Good. And I like Cocoa.

Sigh. Beat in an argument by a 9-year old.

YES VIRGINIA, HE IS A DOG

The other day I was walking my dog. The normal response from the neighborhood kids is to follow me around asking if they can walk Dexter too. This day, as we moved through the park, the crowd of kids slowly thinned out to just a little boy and a little girl, both of whom seemed fascinated by Dexter. The little girl was asking questions and telling me about her cats:

Little Girl: Mr. Policeman, why do you have Dexter on that thing?

Me: What thing?

Little Girl: That thing you're holding.

Me: This is a leash. It keeps him from running away when I bring him outside.

Little Girl: We let our cats out sometimes but we don't put them on one of those things.

Me: Yeah. Cats don't like leashes too much.

Little Girl: What's he looking for?

Me: Probably a place to use the bathroom.

Little Girl: Our cats don't use the bathroom outside. They have a box.

Me: Cats are good like that.

Little Girl: Why do you walk Dexter then?

Me: Dogs aren't so good at learning to use a litter box.

Little Girl, very surprised: You mean he's a dog?

Me: Ahhh, yeah.

Poor dog, even the kids are confused over what species he is.

JUST A QUESTION

One of my neighbors called me with a question. He's a good kid and has been a friend of my department for a number of years now:

Jabari: Hi Wayne, this is Jabari, I have a question for you.

Me: Sure. Go with it.

Jabari: If my mom has insurance on her car, but I don't have insurance on me, can I still legally drive her car?

I pause for a moment. California law requires that the vehicle be insured. Your rates may increase depending on how many licensed drivers are in the household and the age of those drivers, but if the vehicle is insured, then any licensed driver may drive it and be covered by the policy.

Me: What does your mom say?

Jabari: She says I can't drive her car.

Me: Then your mom is right.

Moms are always right.

MOVIE, DINNER, AND A FELONY
ARREST

My girlfriend at the time, also a cop but in a neighboring jurisdiction, and I had gone to see a movie and then out for dinner before returning to my apartment to watch TV for a bit before she went over to her parents' for the night to dog sit. As we were watching the television, there was a pounding at the door. I got up and went to answer it only to find four to five kids all huddled in front of my apartment. They were telling me that some people were fighting. I assumed that it was kids fighting and had actually headed out the door to break it up and send everyone home for the evening when one of the kids told me that the man had threatened, "To kick her ass." I was advised that it sounded like he was beating the woman "pretty hard." This changed my response. Breaking up a fight between kids generally only requires a strong command presence. Intervening in a domestic violence situation requires more equipment. I turned around, opened the door and started to go back inside only to find my girlfriend about ready to go outside. I must have looked confused for a moment because she looked at me and said, "What? You didn't think I was going to stay here did you?"

We got the necessary equipment and went to the apartment where this incident was taking place. After knocking on the door several times it was answered by a woman who had obviously been hit. She was crying and had a bloody lip. I asked if the man was still in the apartment and when she said yes, we entered. The man was in a back room, buck naked. He was advised to show me his hands and to come out of the room. When he complied, I had him sit down on the floor where I could maintain control of him until uniformed officers arrived. As I made my call to my department to request back up units, I calmly told the man that, because I was off-duty, I had limited force options so that gave him three choices. He could be shot, be hit with my expandable baton or he could remain seated on the floor and not cause any problems. While he complained that it was undignified for him to have to sit on the floor in his own house without any clothes on, there he remained until one of my officers arrived and took custody of him.

Once my officers had control of the scene, my girlfriend and I walked back to my apartment. As we walked I had to comment on the evening's activities, "A movie, dinner and an arrest. Have to love a date that ends with a felony pop." She laughed. I had to lament the fact that during the course of the evening she saw a naked man and it wasn't me.

Later, one of my neighbors commented to me regarding the arrest, "Ain't that some shit Sarge. That girl had your back." He stole a furtive glance at his "lady" friend with whom he has had frequent, loud verbal altercations and mumbled, "You don't know how lucky you are."

Oh, I think I do.

I KNOW WHERE YOU LIVE

H aving got off work at 3 am this morning and getting to bed around 4 am, you can imagine that I was a little annoyed when my phone rang at 8:30 am. Reflex kicked in and before my sleep muddled mind could register the fact that I could ignore said phone I had already picked it up, flipped it open and slurred out my typical greeting..."Sergeant Cotes."

Lady: Sergeant Wayne, Sergeant Wayne. There is a stolen car here behind the building and there are some homeless people stripping it and they're fighting over who gets to take the parts and waving tire irons around at each other.

I'm thinking, ohhh, a stolen car, people fighting, tire irons. I don't have to ask what building. Even though my mind hasn't cleared, I recognize her voice and know where to go. Nothing like a little rowdiness to wake you up in the morning, almost as good as coffee. I tell her that I'll be out in a minute, hang up the phone, roll out of bed and put on my off-duty gear which consists of a gun belt and a jacket with pull down "POLICE" identifiers and head out the door.

Apparently, I'm too well known out here. Even out of uniform I'm a block away and can see people messing with the car (the housing complex where I live is several blocks large and this was on the complete opposite side from where my apartment is), when two of the would-be car strippers raise up and spot me. The old saying about no honor among thieves remains true to this day. They immediately start running northbound away from me but neglected to tell their friend that I was approaching. He continues to work diligently at removing whatever part he was working on taking off the car.

I'm within half a block when the lone remaining thief raises up and realizes he's all alone. He looks around and sees me. He also recognizes me. Unfortunately for him, I also recognize him. This is what happens when you live next to a cop. He gets to know you, know your family, and tends to remember these little details. For whatever reason though, he decides to run.

I haven't had my coffee yet so I'm not going to run after him but I do yell out, "Jerome, come back over here."

Jerome: NO!

Me: Jerome, come back over here. You're not in any trouble. (ok, he was in some trouble but unless he had actually removed something from the car he most likely wouldn't go to jail, I know he didn't steal the car as that would require some skill and Jerome is a lot of things but skilled doesn't come to mind as one of them).

Jerome: No! You'll have to do a lot of running to catch me.

"Run?!" I yell back at him across the block's distance that separates us.

Me: Jerome. I don't have to run after you. I know where you live. I know your mama. I can get you later.

He runs any way. I go talk to mom. 20 minutes later, Jerome and I are having a conversation and I never had to break a sweat to catch him. Wish it worked like this all the time.

THE JEDI MIND TRICK

Another favorite tactic of mine is the Jedi Mind Trick. Make people think what you want them to.

There's a place in the east called Greenside that's a heavy drug area. No matter how many people we arrest, or how many stashes we recover, there always seemed to be more. It was frustrating. One day I had been out there several times and each time the result was the same. A large group of dealers would take off running. Fed up, I parked my car, took the yellow chalk that we use for marking the tires of cars we suspect haven't moved in a while and a polaroid camera, and walked to the spot most of the dealers liked to congregate. I began snapping pictures of the surrounding buildings and area and pretended like I was talking on the radio. People were interested and were watching what I was doing. After a few minutes I stood in one spot and got on the radio, "Here?". After a few seconds I would move a few feet left or right and say "here?" into the radio again. When I stopped, I took my piece of yellow chalk and drew a big circle on the ground. As I started to walk away the people watching asked what I was doing. "I'm giving the satellite a position to fix on so that I can watch the drug dealers from a remote location." For the next week, Greenside was quiet.

To clear a corner where there are 7-8 dealers and only one of you, pull out a camera and start taking pictures. If you don't have a camera, use your palm pilot. They'll scatter to the winds.

Other people try the Jedi Mind Trick too. The other day I walked out my back door to clean off my broom and almost tripped over a person sleeping on my back porch.

Me: "Well. Good morning there sunshine."

Person: "Good morning Officer Cotes. Its morning already?"

Me: "Yes, it is. You know who I am and still choose to sleep on my back porch?"

Person: "Yeah. I felt secure."

Me: "Ok. Can't argue there but it's time to go."

As she stands up I hear the distinctive sound of glass clinking off the pavement. We both look down and see the crack pipe that had fallen out of the folds of her clothes laying on the ground.

Person: "You don't see that."

No, I don't suppose I do...

EVALS AND THE COP MENTALITY

My fiance and I recently went through our marriage preparation classes for getting married in the Catholic Church. It was a worthwhile weekend even though my future wife had to work Friday and Saturday night resulting her attending the classes on just a few hours of sleep. It's hard when you get off work at 2 am and then must be in class by 8:30 am but she managed. Better than me as a matter of fact. I think her elbow was getting sore from nudging me awake.

Her being tired does make for some entertaining answers to the questions asked. The way this worked was we would sit through an hour-long presentation and at the end of the presentation the teachers would give us a questionnaire that we would answer on our own and then get together to discuss those answers with our future spouse. Those questions and answers were something like this:

Question: What would help to make your experience here this weekend more beneficial?

Response: A nap.

Question: What would help open the lines of communication between you and your spouse-to-be?

Response: Alcohol.

Question: Would you like to be more creative in your love life and if yes, how would you go about doing so?

Response: Hell yeah! Can you say Karma Sutra?

On Sunday, towards the end of the day, the teachers handed out the class evaluations for us to complete and tell them what we thought about the class.

A little side note about police officers and class evaluations. In the law enforcement community, the class evaluation is handed out at the end of class. That means when you receive it, class is over. It does not mean that you will go through two more segments. That type of thing is strictly forbidden in the cop code of conduct. It's the LAW and you do not mess around with cops and the LAW.

When we got the evaluations to complete, both Jenn and I were glad that class was over. Immediately we start filling them out in an attempt to be on our way home that much quicker. Imagine our shock when we were told that not only did we have to go to a special Mass put on for the participants of the class, but that there was one more segment after Mass that we also had to attend.

I wanted the evaluation back. They obviously did not understand the rules and I wanted to explain it to them. Jenn, being tired, mumbled something about being lucky we were on holy ground.

I'm sure we pouted during the last class. Or maybe not, I was most likely asleep as I distinctly recall Jenn's elbow in my rib cage a few times.

STRANGE CONVERSATIONS

My city just opened up its first Wal-Mart store in August. Why it took so long for a city of 450,000+ people to get one discount store is beyond me. The other day I'm in Wal-Mart getting the oil in my truck changed and picking up a few items. Some of the items I needed were new pillows for my bedroom. I was looking for some pillowcases for them when I was approached by an older man who struck up a conversation.

OM: "New pillows. You're either a bachelor or you're newly married."

Me (smiled): "Neither sir. I'm halfway in between. I'm engaged."

OM: "Oh wonderful. Hope she's a good woman."

Me: "She's the best."

OM: "Glad to hear it. Congratulations."

Me: "Thank you sir."

OM: "How old are you? 25? 26?"

Me (laughing): "No sir. Try 36 but thanks for the compliment."

OM: "36? Really? I would have guessed much younger. I assume you don't have any problems performing."

Me: "Uhhh...."

OM: "What size shoes do you wear?"

Still trying to puzzle out the comment about my "performing", I responded. "These are 11 ½'s."

OM: "Hold out your hand."

My mind at this point hadn't quite caught up to the switch in the conversation so I obediently held out my hand.

OM: "My, my. Look at the size of your hand. You know what that means don't you?"

Me: "That I need big gloves?" (Thanks Adrienne, without you, I'd still be stuck trying to figure out how to respond).

OM: "No, no. They say that there is a correlation between the size of man's feet and hands to the size of his penis."

OK, I saw that one coming. I was hoping it wouldn't, we were, after all, in the middle of Wal-Mart and I was talking with a stranger, but there it was.

Me (lamely): "I've heard that before."

OM: "What are you? Part German?"

Woot! Change of topic and it couldn't have come a moment too soon.

Me: "No. Scottish and Cherokee."

OM: "Oh my. Well, both the Scots and Cherokee are renowned for the size of their penises. Bet you can't wear a kilt."

Damn!

Me: "Didn't know that."

OM: "It's true. So, when did you come out?"

Come out? I wasn't sure what he meant by that. Come out as in "out of the closet?" I'm not gay. Never felt compelled to be in the closet over being straight so I was a tad confused (seemed to be the trend during this encounter.)

Me: "Not sure I follow sir."

OM: "When did you start playing the field?"

Me: "Ahhh, I didn't really start dating dating until I was in my 30's. I wouldn't really call it playing the field though."

OM: "Oh, don't worry about it. I didn't start seeing women till I was older too. No shame in that."

Me: "I discovered women earlier then my 30's sir."

OM (holding up his hand): "Discovered this maybe. No shame in that. Americans have always been prudish about their sexuality compared to Europeans."

Me: "Hmmmm...."

OM: "Well it was nice talking to you and congratulations again on your engagement."

Me: "Ahhh, thank you sir."

Slightly befuddled I shook his hand and watched him walk away. I ran into him later in the service department when he told me that he and his wife had been married for 52 years. He was a nice man, just a strange choice of conversational topics and now he's convinced that I was a 30-year old virgin. I do attract the oddest situations.

LITTLE SLEEP AND NO COFFEE

I had made an appointment to have Dexter, my dog, groomed. Originally, I was thinking that I was working day shift and therefore when the lady gave me an 8:30 am appointment I thought it would be fine. That way I could drop him off before going into work. What I had forgot, was that I was working nightshift the day before. I got to bed at around 3 am. A few hours of sleep, and I stumbled out of bed to take Dex to the groomers.

Perhaps I shouldn't be let out of the house on that little sleep and no coffee. I'm standing there waiting for the shop to open and a lady who is walking down the street see's Dexter.

"OH MY GOD! HOW CUTE!" It was said in the perfect inflection of a Valley Girl accent. She was perky, and bubbly, and I swear to goodness that she bounced and clapped her hands together. I raised an eyebrow. I hated her. "Thanks." I mumbled.

With her hands still pressed together in front of her she bent over and made little baby noises at the dog. He stiffened. He hated her too or maybe he was just picking that up from me. "Oh, he likes me." A big smile.

Likes you? His muscles are so tense you could bend a steel bar across his back. Obviously, the lady isn't very skilled at reading a dog's body language.

Lady: "What kind of dog is he?"

Me: "He's a little dog."

Lady (giggles): "No. I mean what breed?"

I knew what she meant but I was hoping sarcasm would end the conversation. I should have known better. "He's a Moronaranian."

Lady: "Really? I've never heard of that breed."

Me: "Very rare these days, but they were popular in the late 13th Century. They were specially bred for the Sultan of Wisass (pronounced Why-sass) as a unique gift for him to give to his 40 wives."

Lady: "Wow. How fascinating. I have a dog at home that looks just like him. She's just a mixed breed though. A poodle-terrier mix is what the vet said. I named her Baby."

Me: "You would."

Lady: "What?"

Me: "Nothing."

Lady: "Maybe she's a, what did you call it again?"

Me: "He's a Moronaranian. They're in the same family as Pomeranians."

Lady: "Oh, well, that makes sense. Maybe she's one."

Me: "Possibly. It's a common mistake. Check with your vet the next time you take her in."

Lady: "I will. Thank you."

About this time the groomer opens, and I try and make my escape. She bends over again and makes little cooing noises at Dexter and says something about what a cute little boy he is. He bares his teeth. He's not happy about being dragged out of bed for his haircut any more then I am. She thinks he's smiling at her. At least I didn't encourage her to pet him. That would have been negligent.

I shouldn't be allowed out of the house on a few hours of sleep and no coffee. I'm just plain mean.

CAUGHT SPEEDING

One time when I was coming back from Oregon, I was on the phone with one of my corporals discussing work and not really paying attention to my speed. I just happened to glance in my rearview mirror and saw a CHP car pull in behind me. I glanced at my speedometer and realized I was going over the speed limit. I told my corporal that I was being paced by CHP and would probably have to call him back. Right then the CHP officer activated his overheads to do a car stop. I told my corporal I'd call him back and hung up. I put on my hazard lights and pulled smoothly off to the side of the road, turned off my car, took the keys out of the ignition, rolled down the passenger side window and then kept my hands where the officer could see them.

When the CHP officer approached he leaned down to the window and told me that he had pulled me over for speeding. "But I have a question for you."

"Yes sir. Go ahead." I responded.

"Are you a cop?"

Surprised I said yes. "I thought so." He said. "Most people get so unglued when they get pulled over they forget to put the car in park once they stop. You turned on your hazards, pulled off to the side, left me enough room to approach safely on the passenger side and did everything like you knew what the heck you were doing. I wasn't going to write you a ticket anyway but please slow down and have a nice day."

I thanked for his time and told him to be safe. Once I was back on the freeway (and doing the correct speed) I called my corporal back.

Corporal: "I hope this isn't your first phone call Sarge. I don't have the money to bail you out of jail."

OFF-DUTY WORK

In addition to my full-time job as a police officer, I also work an off-duty job at the local sports stadium. It's a great side job to have. You assist the concession stand and area managers with business and get to catch a little of the game. At the end of the game, once the stands have shut down, we make our final rounds. My partner and I were standing next to the ice cream stand as the stand manager finished up with his inventory. A man came up wanting some ice cream and was politely told by the manager that the stand was closed. Judging by the watery eyes, slightly slurred speech and unsure balance, the man was clearly drunk. Slowly he turns towards me:

Man: This is stupid. Is this policy?

Me: Yes sir. It's always been the policy that at the end of the game they close the stands.

Man: Why? People going to get drunk on the ice cream?

Me: It's the sugar sir. It makes people do odd things if they have too much.

Man: What about the odd things that people do if they don't get the sugar?

Me: That generally only happens if they've had too much alcohol.

Man: Are you saying I'm drunk?

Me: Are you going to do odd things if you don't get some ice cream?

Man: I might.

Me: Then you might be drunk.

Man: You think I'm drunk. I can prove that I'm not.

Me: I don't have a breathalyzer on me at the moment sir.

Man: What's that?

Me: Never mind.

Man: I can take a test.

Me: Like a field sobriety test?

Man: Yes. One of those.

Me: Would you stand on one foot and hop up and down while going in circles with your head tilted back?

Man: No.

Me: Then maybe you're not as drunk as I thought you were but you're still not getting any ice cream.

Man. This is stupid. Is this policy?

Me: No sir. This is where we started.

MINI-RANT

I'll be the first person to admit that I work too much. On the days I work night shift, I generally go in to work no later than 3 pm in the afternoon and get out at 2 am. When I work dayshift, I go in at 9 am and usually go off duty somewhere around 7 pm. Most days, I'm only scheduled for a 9-hour shift but consistently work 10 or more (and because I'm considered management, there is no such thing as paid OT). I'm not opposed to taking work-related phone calls during my off-duty hours. I frequently patrol the complex where I live several times a day, even on my weekends but even I have limits.

This past week I was on "vacation." I intentionally use the quotes because the first two evenings of my vacation I spent doing work related things. On Thursday night, I got a phone call from a family that lives in the same complex as I do. I've known their son since he was a kid. He used to participate in our annual PAL (Police Activities League) camps where we take kids from public housing camping for a few days. As he got older, he joined us as a mentor and chaperone. He works hard, stays out of trouble and is the kind of person every parent wants their kids to grow up to be. His family has taken on the responsibility of being foster parents for one of their nephews and he has some issues but is basically a good kid too. This night he had been smoking something he shouldn't have been, and they asked me for my assistance in talking to him. For them, I don't mind and got up out of bed and went over there. They had also called OPD. When the two uniformed officers show up, there I am sitting in the living room in my sweats, a t-shirt and my grungy tennis shoes. One of the officers says, "Hey, you look familiar. Have I arrested you before?" Uh...no. I introduce myself making him a tad uncomfortable.

On Friday night though, my next-door neighbors were having one of their famous throw downs. The father knocks on my door. "Larry is acting all crazy again." No kidding. Larry is 24 years old and thinks that if he just acts stupid enough, the federal government will take pity on him and give him a disability check every month. He's smoked things that by all rights should have killed him (and in fact collapsed one of his lungs not that long ago). Apparently, Larry wanted to watch TV and when his younger brother didn't want to change the channel, Larry decided that if he couldn't watch TV, then no one could. He stole all the cables. In I walk. Larry and his brother are in the kitchen engaged in a tug-a-war over the TV cables. I wrestle the cables away from the two of them and ask what's happening. As I listen, I put the cables down. This prompts the younger brother to reach for them which prompts Larry to try to take them away, which starts the fist fight that I find myself in middle of, on my vacation, when I should be relaxing in my apartment and entertaining my guests. The father has conveniently disappeared. I stop the fight and send everyone to their rooms. Could they stay there and be quiet for the rest of the evening? Of course not. That would make sense and in Larry's world, if it flies in the face of common sense then that is the path he will take. He hits his younger brother. This prompts much holding of face and requests for ice and forces me to have to call for uniformed officers. They take Larry away.

Bah. Next time I go on vacation and stay at home, I'm hiding my car, pulling down all my shades, turning off the lights and pretending I don't exist to the outside world.

DAD

Jack is one of those people who, until his recent retirement, had been in law enforcement for longer than I've been alive. I didn't realize how old he was until one day, still new to the department, Jack and I were partnered up on a special operation. During the low points of the op we would sit and talk. He mentioned about when he first started in police work, in 1968 (or somewhere around there). I had to stop the conversation for a moment while I confirmed how old he was. In Jack's favor, he doesn't look like a man in his 60's despite the gray hair. I know his wife too, and she doesn't look near old enough to be married to a man in his sixties. I was surprised to learn that Jack was older than my parents.

Over the years this became a running joke with me. Once, he and I were discussing bilingual pay and he mentioned that he wished he spoke a second language. I responded back, "You do. Geezer."

I made sure to mention that at his retirement party.

Jack and I also work an off-duty job together. The other day we had just finished our runs and had taken a seat to watch the game until our next round. A man sitting behind us caught our attention and then asked if we were father and son. I just laughed. Nick's response was just a little tepid as he told the man no.

Once the inning was over we got up to continue with our duties. When the elevator door opened, Jack stepped off to the side and with an eloquent gesture said, "After you son." I insisted that "Dad" go first. We should, after all, treat our elders with respect.

As the door to the elevator closed I smiled and looked at Nick. "Don't feel too bad Nick, at least the man thought you were handsome enough to be my father."

He smiled and said, "I just can't believe that they thought you were handsome enough to be my son."

Touché.

NOT A DOCTOR

Prior to living in that little piece of heaven my city calls "The 85th Ville", I was the resident of a small town about 75 miles from where I worked. When I first moved out there I kept my line of work a secret as it usually results in someone asking why that evil police officer wrote them a speeding ticket when they were only going 80 in a 65 mph zone. That generally resulted in me pointing out the obvious and pissing people off so when I moved to Patterson, my profession was my business…initially any way, eventually someone finds out and the odd questions and requests begin.

My neighbor, Lisa, and her family were nice but a little off. I remember working in the back yard one day when she was yelling at her two sons about why they were always arguing and why they couldn't get along. "You two never fight when you're high on weed. Why can't you be like that all the time?" I suppose her intent was, why couldn't they get along all the time like they did when they were high on weed but I couldn't help but wonder if she weren't encouraging them to be doped up more regularly.

So, one day I'm sitting in my family room watching TV when there's a frantic beating at the door. I got up and when I opened the front door I found Lisa standing there with one of her son's friends. The friend was crying and had one hand covering his right eye.

Me: "What happened?" (I have a tendency to bypass the pleasantries in certain situations and get right down to business).

Lisa (somewhat frantic): "Steven and his friend were playing and Steven shot him in the eye with a BB gun. Do something."

Me: "I can call an ambulance if you want."

Lisa: "You can't take it out?"

Me: "Uh, no."

Lisa: "But you're a cop. Aren't you trained for these kinds of things? First aid or something?"

Me: "If you've stopped breathing I know CPR. If you have a stab wound, I know to put pressure on it till paramedics arrive. No stab wound and he looks to be breathing just fine. BB in the eye is a little past my skill set Lisa. I'm a police officer, not a doctor."

Lisa: "You can't do anything?"

Me: "Sure. Just let me grab my pocketknife, a lighter and a bottle of whiskey and I'll pop that eye right out. Hmmm, maybe I better grab a tourniquet too; just in case the whiskey makes my hands unsteady and I sever an artery or something."

Lisa: "Ok."

My sarcasm apparently lost on her in the heat of the moment I told her I'd be right back.

Me: "Hello 911? Yes, my neighbor's son shot another kid in the eye with a BB gun and she's at my door thinking I can pop the BB out with a pocketknife sterilized by a lighter. I'm thinking that would be a bad idea. Could you send a paramedic unit please? Yes, I'll hold. Thank you."

LINE UP QUIPS AND QUOTES

Cops are, by nature, somewhat sarcastic (I'm being nice). Throw a bunch of us in a room together and there are bound to be some snappy comebacks.

LINE UP PART 1

What's more commonly called roll call is what we call line up.
During line-up after I made a mistake on the watch log.
Me: "Jose, you have some whiteout?"
Jose: "No. I don't make mistakes."
Brandon: "You don't write reports either."

AT THE END OF LINE UP

Me: Anyone have any questions?
Ramon: I have one Sarge.
Me (with a sigh): Go ahead Ramon.
Ramon: Why I am I so damn good looking?

DURING LINE-UP

Rich: Except for Cotes, at 37, I'm the oldest guy here.
Me: Wait a minute, I'm only 32.
Rich: Only 32? Sorry boss, but life has been a little rough on you.

DURING INSPECTION

Me: Rod, where's your radio mike?
Rod: I took it off. It made me sound sarcastic.
Me: A radio mike did that?
Rod: Well, it certainly isn't me.

DURING INSPECTION II

Me: You have food on your shirt.
Bruce: Sorry, that's my breakfast.
Me: Can't you keep it in your mouth like everyone else?

AT THE END OF LINE-UP II

Me: Any questions?
Ramon: Yeah Sarge. Just one. Why am I so good looking?
Me: Ok, who stopped payment on Ramon's reality check?

LINE UP PART 2

Recently, one of my officers, was on his way to morning line-up and was suffering from cranial-rectal inversion when he ran a red light and got hit by two vehicles from the opposing lanes of traffic. Two cars (including one of ours) were totaled. The other vehicle, a pickup truck belonging to the school district, was seriously damaged, and there was a building that was also damaged.

During line-up that morning, the investigations unit supervisor and one of his officers were returning from an early morning meeting at the City and were a few minutes late to line-up.

Officer 1 (the one who ran the red light): Oh, nice of you to show up to line-up.

Investigator: Yeah. It was those damn traffic lights slowing me down. I actually had to stop for one.

LINE UP PART 3

During line-up, the Executive Director was there to present a 5-year pin to our investigation unit's administrative assistant. At the conclusion of the presentation he asked if any of us had any questions so I raised my hand.

Me: Yes, John was wondering when our medical plan was going to cover Rogaine treatments?

Jim: And Wayne would like to know when the prescription benefit will cover Viagra.

OK, I deserved that…

DOORS, PUBLIC ENEMY
NUMBER ONE

One of my officers, getting into his patrol car one day after clearing a call, neglected to get his head out of the way as he shut the door. End result, several stitches to close up the laceration left by the corner of the door.

During a separate incident, the exit from our station is down a hallway. You make a short right-hand turn, go down three steps and there's the door. Now this door has one of the push bars on it that is used to open it. Glen was headed out with me right behind him. He took the stairs, hit the push bar and....well, someone had locked the deadbolt, so the door didn't open. SMACK!! Glen ran into that door hard. He took a step back and sat down heavily on the stairs. It took a while before I could stop laughing hard enough to ask him if he was ok. End result, concussion.

While serving an arrest warrant with the municipal police department, the subject of the warrant was confirmed to be inside but was refusing to answer the door. I asked if anyone had a "key" (a small, portable battering ram). One officer said we didn't need a key and proceeded to wind up to kick the door in. I tried to explain it was a steel core door, really I did....

End result, stress fractures.

COURT TESTIMONY

In my city, the big drugs of choice are rock cocaine, heroin and marijuana. While I've made some rather large busts for LSD and Ecstasy, those were mostly during the days of the Grateful Dead concerts. In court, I have been certified as an expert witness in the possession for sale of our three biggest drugs of choice.

On December 31, 1996, at 3:30 pm, I was in court for a preliminary exam on an arrest I had made for both powder cocaine and meth. While I had never been certified as an expert witness in either, powder cocaine was easy. I had made a number of arrests for the possession, possession for sale, or sales of that drug and was familiar with sales techniques, lingo, packaging, etc. Meth on the other hand was a whole different story. At the time, I had only made 3 arrests for meth and that included the one I was in court on.

The District Attorney went through his questions and I answered the best I could. When he was done, he sat down with a heavy sigh realizing that in this area, as an expert witness, I was far from ideal. The judge asked the defense if they had any additional questions and the defense tore into me, primarily on the number of arrests.

Public Defender: "Your Honor, I move that Officer Cotes not be submitted as an expert witness in the possession of methamphetamines for sale. He clearly lacks the knowledge in this area to be certified as such."

Judge: "Do you know what day it is?"

Public Defender: "Yes, your Honor. It's New Year's Eve."

Judge: "Do you know what time it is?"

131

Public Defender: "Yes."

Judge: "Will you concede that Officer Cotes knows more about the possession for sales of methamphetamine then the average person?"

Public Defender (sarcastically): "No your Honor. Heck, my client knows more about that then the officer does."

Judge: "Really?"

Public Defender: "Errrr...that's not what I meant. I just meant that my client, with his lack of experience in this area would be more qualified to testify as an expert witness than Officer Cotes."

Judge: "Would you like that to be a part of the record councilor?"

PD: "No your Honor."

Judge: "I thought not. Please strike Mr. Rice's last two comments from the record please. Now, Mr. Rice, do you have any further questions for Officer Cotes before I make my ruling on this matter?"

PD: "No your Honor."

Judge: "Then, in my court, Officer Cotes is an expert witness in the possession of methamphetamines for sale."

For the rest of the preliminary hearing, the public defender refused to say anything. The defendant was held to answer and remanded back into custody.

Amazing what can be accomplished late in the afternoon on New Year's Eve.

LOOKING FOR DAN AND OTHER AWKWARDNESS

After eleven years with our department, Officer Dan Jones has retired and moved on to other things. I would call moving to Bakersfield "other things." I remember when Dan was first hired. I was 24-years old at the time, and only a year or two out of the Marine Corps. Dan had just retired from the Navy after 23 years and was looking to get started on his second career. I'm sure during his tenure as a Sailor, that he had dealt with any number of young, hard-nosed Marines. Just never one that was his Field Training Officer. Despite having spent all those years in the Navy, he turned out to be one of the best officers to ever wear our badge. When he was hired, the Chief told me that, with Dan being older, he would bring some needed maturity to a very young department. The Chief was right of course but it also provided me with years of jokes about his age.

On Thursday, we had his retirement party. The Police Officers' Association picked a good location and it was a nice party. By the time I was done conducting training at what has affectionately been referred to as "Tassa Dojo", named after the complex it was in, Dan and a number of other people were already there. I took a seat and was carrying on a conversation with one of the people from Resident and Community Services when our dispatcher, Allie, walked in with the cake. After setting the cake on the table, she was standing near me and looking right at Dan. Actually, let me correct that, she was looking in Dan's direction but apparently didn't see him. Her asking when Dan was going to arrive prompted the reason I differentiate between the two statements. I look at Dan, and then look at Allie, before saying,

"He should be here pretty quick. When he walks in, we're all going to yell surprise. Would you do me a favor and go stand by the door and tell us when he comes in?"

"Sure Sarge." Allie goes and stands by the door and every few seconds, spurred on by me constantly asking if he's coming yet, looks towards the front of the restaurant. Other people catch on and start adding their own comments. Things like, "He should be coming in Class A's Allie," and, "Make sure he doesn't see you." This continued until Dan finally asked me who it was Allie was waiting on. "You." I replied. Dan ruined our amusement by telling Allie he was already there and had been since she walked through the door.

That fun being done with I continue to mingle with the people there and notice a young lady who had hereto escaped my notice. I remember her distinctly as one member of a group of juveniles that were party to a large fight and assault on 72nd Avenue not that long ago. When told to leave the property they wanted to lecture me on how this was "their neighborhood" and they could go where they wanted. They didn't leave. That was a day and a time when it wasn't good to try and tell me what you will and won't do particularly when what I needed you to do was move and what you want to do is stay.

One of the things I learned early on in my career is that I don't carry enough handcuffs to hook up everyone in these types of situations. The other thing I learned is that I don't have to. One person will usually suffice as a message to everyone else. When I started walking towards the group, the group started backing away and she was the slowest. As a result, she got to spend some time in the rear seat of a patrol car. Amazingly, the rest of the group dispersed. Mission accomplished.

Turns out she is the granddaughter of an employee and here she was at the retirement party. Could be a little awkward. I don't generally like to socialize with people that I've put handcuffs on in an official capacity but it's not my party and Mr. Community Policing, Jason Willis, was over talking to her. After he carries on a brief conversation with her he comes over to me and asks if I remember her and tells me that she remembers me as "Robo-cop." I'm not sure how that reference applies to me but I'm sure that it isn't a positive comparison. I tell him that I do remember, and he motions her over. I introduce myself as Wayne figuring that not using official titles may make things go a little smoother. To my surprise, she turns out to be a very pleasant young lady.

I'll miss Dan. He's a great officer and an excellent investigator. More than that though, he had that rare combination of being older than me and having been a Sailor. That kind of joke material is very hard to replace.

CHOKE DEFENSE

Every week a small group of my officers and supervisors go through weaponless defense training. This training includes hand-to-hand combat, self-defense, arrest control and compliance, searching and ground fighting. In this particular class, we were working on a self-defense technique for being choked.

I was working with a group of students when I hear one of the other students make a weird kind of uggghh-ouch noise. I look over and see John rubbing his neck.

Me: You ok?

John (continuing to rub his neck): Yeah.

Me: What happened?

John: He choked me.

Well, yeah, that is kind of the point of the exercise.

ROOKIES

One thing I always wanted to do to a rookie fresh out of the academy and brand new to the Field Training Program.

Me: "Only one thing you need to remember."

Joe (rookie): "What?"

Me: "If I ever call you by the wrong name I want you to shoot whoever we are talking to. Got that Rob? It is Rob isn't it?"

MIS-SPEAKS

Yesterday, Ramon and I were conducting weaponless defense training with a few of the officers. In addition to the standard arrest control techniques, control holds, takedowns, etc., we also teach Krav Maga, the Israeli self-defense/hand-to-hand combat system. We had been covering personal weapons and defenses and Ramon was explaining to one of the students how over-extending his blocks leaves him open to counter-attacks.

Ramon: When you over-extend your arm here, you're open here and BAM!, I can hit you with the left cross. If you over-extend your arm this way then you're open here and BAM!, I can hit you with the right cross. See, either way I can hit you with the opposite hand. Now, not everyone trains with both hands but I'm amphibious so I'm cool like that.

Like myself, Ramon is a former Marine and there is a part of our un-official creed that goes, "I am a green, amphibious monster made of blood and guts who arose from the sea, festering on anti-Americans throughout the globe." So, yeah, I'll give him the amphibious part out of respect for our shared Marine Corps heritage but I'm positive that's not what he meant.

In his defense, Ramon did claim to have read that in a magazine and thought it was funny, so he used it; unlike an officer I heard about in a neighboring jurisdiction who, when faced with the possibility of disciplinary action, called in sick by saying he had "ammonia."

Yeah, ok, lay off the smelling salts boss and that should clear right up.

THE LONG DRIVE HOME

When I lived out in the central valley, it was a long commute back and forth every day. 150 miles round trip, although as the police car flies, I could cut that down to only a little over an hour each way (barring traffic congestion which on a Friday night usually meant I left the station at 6 and didn't get home till around 8:30 to 9 pm at night). Even though I was in a police car, as previously mentioned, it was an unmarked vehicle, so most people didn't pay any attention to me. This was fine in my book. I was off duty and unless it was a matter of public safety, I didn't really care if you were speeding. Nonetheless, there were times when people would annoy the hell out of me...

One day I was on my way home and was moving along at a nice clip of about 75 mph (the posted speed limit was 70 mph so I wasn't going that far over) when a sedan comes zooming up behind me in the other lane, passes me and then, without signaling to let me know he was coming over, changes lanes to pass a car in his lane, about 2 feet from my front bumper causing me to brake hard to make sure there wasn't an inadvertent collision. The Marine in me creeps up to the surface and there was a string of cursing that would have made a DI nod his head with approval.

You don't always realize the influence your mother has on you (if you have a great relationship with her like I do with mine). Somewhere in the back of my mind I hear my mom's voice telling me, "You know they can't hear you."

Growing up, my dad, also a former Marine, had this particular habit of yelling at people when we were driving from Ellicott into town

(town being Colorado Springs, Ellicott wasn't a town, it was a blip on the radar that occupied four corners of the road. On one corner was the gas station, the other the blacksmith shop, then the ranch headquarters for one of the big ranchers in the area, and then someone's house, probably the guy who owned the gas station). My mom would always tell him, "Sam, you know they can't hear you, but the kids can." This, generally speaking, had a calming influence on my dad who would remain silent until the next person annoyed him and the whole scene would replay itself (of course there was that time he said, "I don't know what the hell I'm doing out here with all the other idiots on the road." which started a running commentary from the back seat, said with all innocence, how I didn't think that my father was an idiot at all which turned my dad's full attention to me and started a conversation going back and forth that eventually had my mom giving us the LOOK - the LOOK is capitalized for a reason, only moms have it, perfected by years of disciplining children in public places where a backhand would just be considered uncivilized).

The echo of my mom's voice in my head made me chuckle as I reminisced. Still, this guy had cut me off and how I wished that he could hear me...oh wait, I'm in a police car, I have a PA. I speed up as I pick up the mic and blaring out across I-5 comes the that slightly mechanical voice that can only be done with a voice amplification device.

"SIR, YOU IN THE GRAY CAR. YES YOU, THE ONE WHO CUT OFF A POLICE CAR. THERE IS A LEVER ON THE LEFT SIDE OF YOUR STEERING COLUMN. IT'S CALLED A BLINKER AND IT'S USED TO LET OTHER DRIVERS KNOW WHEN YOU ARE CHANGING LANES. LEARN IT. LOVE IT. USE IT LIKE YOUR DRIVING PRIVILEGES DEPENDED ON IT BECAUSE THEY DO."

The driver is looking up in the rearview mirror with a look somewhere between disbelief and guilt. He slows down to 65 mph. Just to ensure that my message came across loud and clear, I stay behind him. He continues to do 65 mph for the next 20 miles and every time we passed a truck, he used his blinker.

My job here is done.

AWWWW

One day, I had stopped in at my favorite Chinese restaurant to have lunch. The place really doesn't look like much, but it has great food.

When I walked in, there was a lady sitting there with what appeared to be her mother and her 4-year old son. As soon as I walked in the little boy was pulling on his mom's sleeve and saying, "Look mommy, a police man." He then waved at me, "Hi Mr. Policeman."

I waved back, grabbed a newspaper off the counter and took a seat. I come here often enough that the owner generally just asks me if I want my usual (Mongolian Beef with Fried Rice, mmmmm, good).

While I'm sitting there reading the newspaper the little boy tells his mom, "Mommy, you know what I want to be when I grow up? I want to be a policeman just like him." And he points at me.

I smile (ok, it was more of a grin, but he was so cute and was making me feel pretty special).

After a while, the lady, her mom, and her son have finished up their meal, but they are sitting and talking and the little boy is wandering a little and comes up to me. He tells me that he wants to be a police officer when he grows up and I tell him how wonderful that would be and that we need all the help we can get before his mom calls him back to the table and they get up to leave. I wave bye, finish up the last of my lunch and also get up to leave.

I'm standing in line right behind the little boy and his family. As they start to walk out the door, the little boy turns and says, "Bye Mr. Policeman." and waves at me. I wave back and tell him bye.

The little boy is out the door when he turns around and runs back to me and wraps his arms around my leg in a hug and says in his little boy voice, "I love you Mr. Policeman." He then runs back out to his mom.

I'll risk being labeled a sap and admit that I melted. Made my day though.

A MARINE STORY

My partner, who I will refer to as my brother for the sake of telling this story, and I went to boot camp together on the buddy program. Even growing up together, we had two completely different lifestyles. I maintained good grades, participated in sports and generally tried not give my parents too much of a hassle. My brother on the other hand screwed off in school to the point where I had to take him in early to make up classes and he had to stay late in order to graduate. At one point, he had been into the drug scene. While he had never been an addict, there was little he didn't experiment with. This included LSD.

At the end of each day in boot camp, after you had showered and shaved and were ready to hit the rack right before taps, the drill instructor would conduct a hygiene inspection. Everyone would stand on their foot lockers and the DI would walk down the aisle and make sure that you had trimmed your toe nails, cleaned behind your ears, shaved properly, etc.

Like I said, we went to boot camp together and so our bunks were right above/below one another's. It's time for hygiene inspection and Drill Instructor Sergeant Yoyo is inspecting my brother with me being next, when my brother giggles and says in a high pitched, squeaky voice, "Bubbles. What pretty bubbles."

The other thing about brother you need to know is that, outside of our Senior Drill Instructor (who was a 6'7" tall, albino looking hardass), he was the tallest person in our platoon at 6'5". Imagine a man that big giggling and talking about bubbles.

Imagine the look on Drill Instructor Sergeant Yoyo's face when a man that big giggles and talks about the pretty bubbles. It was a classic cross between complete shock and total disbelief.

Yoyo whips around on my brother:

Yoyo: "Private Corpland, what the f*ck did you just say?"

My brother, still lost in his own little world, doesn't respond, he just sits there with a goofy grin on his face staring into the space.

Yoyo: "Private Cotes! What the f*ck did Private Corpland just say?"

Me: "Sir, Private Cotes believes that Private Corpland giggled, sir, and said, oh what pretty bubbles. Sir."

Side note: Use of the pronoun "I" in boot camp would earn you a good ass chewing and some time in the pit and was usually followed up by the DI who overheard it, making such comments as, "I? I? There are no I's in the Corps private. Say it again and I'll gouge yours out, throw them in the pit and you can sift through the dirt saying, eye? Got it?" Use of the word "you" generally earned you even more colorful commentary regarding sheep but I'll save that one.

Now at this point, I am trying really hard not to laugh. It was hard enough hearing him say it, but to have to repeat it almost broke my discipline and sent me into a fit of hysterics.

Yoyo whips back on my brother, "Private Corpland, what the f*ck is your major malfunction?" No response but he's starting to come around. Yoyo whips back on me, "Private Cotes, what the f*ck is wrong with Private Corpland?"

Me: "Sir. Private Cotes believes Private Corpland may be having a flash back. Sir."

Yoho, whipping back to my brother (DI's have mastered the art of whipping around on people. One minute they are doing one thing and the next, without seeming to really move, they are in your face): "Private Corpland this is boot camp! The United States Marine Corps' boot camp and you do not have permission to take a vacation into whatever la-la land your brain housing group has wandered into. Snap to private and get your overgrown ass to the DI hut now. Move!"

Proof positive that several months of intensive training can overcome even a drug induced flash back, my brother hustles off to the DI's office. Dazed, not sure what the heck he did to earn himself this pleasure, but off he double times.

OFFICE BOY

One of our officers had developed a problem with his plumbing and as a result he was placed on light duty status for several weeks while he recovered. His duties during this time included administrative and office duties around the station. I had affectionately started calling him "Office Boy," and would make comments like, "You're out of uniform today Glen. No pocket protector." Or, if he was walking out of the Chief's office tell him to wipe off his chin or ask him if kneepads were standard issued equipment for his position like vests were for real cops or if he had to buy his own. You know, general harassment.

One day we had a ride-along. Some kid, fresh out of the academy who was wanting to apply for a position with our department. He was selected to ride with me. As part of the process, we go through and introduce the ride-along to everyone who's working that day. I don't actually recall saying anything specifically about Glen when he was introduced, but later on when we sat down for lunch, the ride-along was asking questions:

Ride-along: Hey, what's up with that one officer?

Me: What one officer?

Ride-along: Hmmmm, I can't remember his name but it was that guy upstairs. You know, Office Boy.

I about fell out.

INTERVIEWS

During my first interview for the position of police officer, I was being asked scenario questions by two older police officers who looked as if their faces had been carved out of stone. One of the scenario questions had to do with a person running a stop sign and what I would do.

Officer: You are conducting traffic enforcement on a stop sign that you have received numerous complaints about. As you're watching, a vehicle runs the stop sign. You conduct a traffic stop and approach the driver and get his driver's license and registration. What action are you going to take?

Me: I'd issue him a citation.

Officer: Why?

Me: Well, I was there specifically to conduct traffic enforcement because of complaints I had received.

Officer: Ok. Same situation only this time as you approach, it's the Mayor of this city. What would you do?

Me: Issue him a citation.

Officer: You would issue the Mayor a ticket?

Me: Yes.

Officer: This is the Mayor of this city. He would go to the Chief, your boss, and want to know why you had issued him a ticket. This could have political implications. Would you still issue him the ticket?

Me: Yes.

Officer: You understand that you have discretion, right? You don't have to write the Mayor a ticket.

Me: Yes.

Officer: But you would still issue him a citation.

Me: Yes (start to see a pattern here).

Officer: Why?

Me: As the elected leader of this city I feel that he should not only be held to the same standard as the citizens but to a higher standard. How would it look to the populace if I issued them a ticket but let the Mayor off with a warning?

Officer: I see. Same situation but this time it's, (looking at my application), Sam Cotes. Who is Sam Cotes?

Me: That's my father.

Officer: I see here that he lives in Colorado.

Me: Yes.

Officer: Ok. Your father runs the stop sign and you pull him over. What would you do?

Me: Ask him what the hell he was doing in California.

Leaden stares and dead silence.....

Note to self: Humor on an oral board is a bad thing

Note to readers: I got that job.

While conducting interviews for the position of police officer, one question that's asked is regarding drug possession. You can't ask a person how many times they've used drugs, that's forbidden under the American's with Disabilities Act (ADA), but you can ask them how many times they've possessed drugs which is a violation of law.

Interviewer: How many times have you possessed illegal drugs? And mind you that passing the joint around while you're sitting with your friends constitutes possession.

Lady wishing to be a police officer: I don't know. I experimented some with drugs.

Interviewer: When was the first time you possessed drugs?

Lady: Oh, about 1989.

Interviewer: When was the last time you possessed drugs?

Lady: Oh, about 1991 (mind you this was 1992).

Interviewer: Ok, between 1989 and 1991, about how many times did you possess drugs?

Lady: I don't know, a couple of thousand times maybe.

Interviewer: Ok. Thank you.

Note to Lady: A couple of thousand times possessing drugs in a two-year period isn't experimentation, its addiction.

During another interview with an applicant, the same question was asked. He responded by saying that he once grew a few marijuana plants for personal use and wondered if that constituted possession.

Interviewer: Yes it does. How many plants did you have?

Applicant: About 600.

Interviewer: Ok. Thank you.

Note to Applicant: 600 plants is a grow operation, not personal use.

TRAINING

During a recent training session, we were going through forward and reverse strikes with our impact weapons (batons). The focus of the training was to deliver one forward and one reverse strike against an instructor holding a large strike pad, give your "suspect" a command and then pause to assess whether you were having the desired affect (i.e. the suspect is complying with your commands to quit resisting and submits to the arrest). We did this exercise multiple times in a row, going forward and backwards through the training area.

During one student's run through of this exercise:

Forward step, strike, strike...

Student: "Sir, get down on the ground. Quit resisting!"

Pause, forward step, strike, strike...

Student: "Sir, get down on the ground. Quit resisting!"

Pause, forward step, strike, strike....

Student: "Sir, get down on the ground. Quit resisting!"

Pause, backwards step, strike, strike...

Student: "Sorry about your arm sir. Get down. Quit resisting!"

Pause, backwards step, strike, strike...

Student: "We'll pick it up on the way back sir. Get down and quit resisting!"

Pause, backwards step, strike, strike...

Student: "Sir, get down on the ground. Quit resisting!"

It was good for a chuckle.

COMPUTERS

I was sitting at my desk going over an evaluation when my phone rings...

Me: Sergeant Cotes.

Dispatcher: Hey Sarge, Kevin says that Client 4 is running slow and would like you to reset it.

Client 4 is the program that connects our laptop computers in the patrol cars to the main server for our dispatch center.

Me (jokingly): Tell him to flip the actuator switch on his computer and put it into hyper-drive, that will make it run faster. In the meantime, I'll reset Client 4.

Dispatcher: Ok.

I hang up the phone and start to head upstairs when I hear over our alternate channel...

Kevin: 16L4 on two.

Dispatch: Per 16L75, he wants you to flip the actuator switch on your computer and put it into hyper-drive. He says that will make it run faster.

Kevin (after a long pause): 10-4 (acknowledged).

When my phone rings again, I'm almost laughing too hard to get my name out and Kevin is right there with me.

REVENGE OF THE DISPATCHER

I'm sitting at my desk attacking the malignant pile of paperwork on my desk that never seems to diminish, when my dispatcher calls me.

Me: Sergeant Cotes.

Dispatch: Hey Sarge, can you help me out and pick up 3100?

Me: Sure.

I hang up and pick up the other line. I know from the slow drawl of the voice that it's Mr. Garth.

Mr. Garth is what's known in the business as a 5150. This is the code for a person who is socially misaligned. In less politically correct and more common vernacular, he's nutty as peanut butter.

He's calling to complain that his landlord (he's on Section 8) is in violation of Fair Housing standards because she told him he needed to take a bath more often. He then admitted that he hadn't taken a bath in five months and that it had been necessary just in case his landlord decided she didn't like Section 8, he wouldn't feel compelled to call her up and threaten to blow up the building. He was fairly adamant that he didn't want to do that and that taking a bath was his insurance. I'd be curious to know how that insures him from calling and making threats but one thing I've learned with Mr. Garth is that you don't ask questions that may prolong the conversation any further. What took me only a minute to type, took him 30 minutes to say.

I thank him for keeping me informed and tell him to have a good day before hanging up the phone and heading up stairs to have a chat with the dispatcher about setting me up. She's snickering just as soon as I walk through the door into the communications center.

Dispatcher: Enjoy your conversation Sarge?

Me: That was wrong. You know it was wrong. I wouldn't mind so much if he didn't talk so slow.

Dispatch (with a straight face): Did you try flipping his actuator switch and putting him in to hyper-drive? Might make him talk faster.

Check. Paybacks are hell aren't they.

WE'RE NOT THE ONLY ONES

J ust to show that my department isn't the only one with a somewhat warped sense of humor:

I was attending a multi-jurisdictional meeting where we were discussing crime trends in various hot spots throughout our respective areas. A command officer from another agency was advising of an armed robbery where a prostitute climbed into a taco truck, put a knife to the victim's neck and told him to hand over all his money. An inquisitive deputy chief asked how the prostitute managed to get into the back of a taco truck when the trucks are usually locked. This prompted several hypotheses all of which speculated on the victim inviting the prostitute in for the exchange of favors. Someone piped in with a nice catch phrase, "Perhaps a little quid pro ho."

At another meeting, we were discussing a small person who worked as a prostitute on one of the main drags in my city. One of the deputies attending the meeting piped in and said that her street name was "Half-price."

HAZARDS OF THE JOB

One of my officers was performing a pat search for officer safety. When he bent down to check around his detainee's ankles for weapons he heard the distinct sound of the detainee breaking wind followed by the a somewhat noxious odor. While the detainee claimed that scar tissue on his back made it difficult for him to control his flatulence, I maintain that he waited until the officer's head was only a few inches away from waist level. Hazards of the job (also a certain amount of justice as this same officer has ran several of us out of the locker room with his "stomach" problems).

A MILITARY MYSTERY

When I was in the Marine, the Enlisted Club was within stumbling distance of the barracks. We used to crack jokes about them putting the two Marine Corps detachments on the base closest to the alcohol. The E-Club was a regular Friday and Saturday night hangout for most of us. It was right before the holidays and I was scheduled to leave for Colorado the following day and wanted to make sure I had time to pack so I choose to go home after only having a couple of beers. I wasn't even close to being drunk. Let me repeat that before you continue reading...I WAS NOT DRUNK. It wasn't late, only around 2300 hours (11 P.M for you non-military types). I got undressed and crawled up into my rack (bed). I shared a room with one other person. The beds were bunk style but sat above a desk instead of another bed. The fact that my bed sits up high becomes a key piece of evidence shortly.

The following morning I was woken from my peaceful sleep by the sound of a toilet flushing. Now, a toilet flushing in and of itself wouldn't be unusual except that we didn't have a head (bathroom) in our room. Such luxuries were reserved for our more pampered counter parts in the Navy. I ignored it thinking that I must be dreaming. I squeezed my eyes shut a little tighter, pulled the covers up over the top of my head and attempted to drift back off to sleep. I'm just starting to drift back off when I hear the unmistakable sound of water running in a shower. Once again, this wouldn't be unusual if it weren't for the fact that my room had no bathroom and therefore no shower. My sleep muddled mind attempted to work out the incongruities of these events by telling itself that I must be hearing the water running from the communal head I shared with the barracks 80 other occupants. Even half asleep though I quickly dismissed this theory given the location of the head (down the hall, to the left and down a little further) in relation to my room.

About this time is when that little sneaky feeling that something is wrong or out of place starts to grow larger with each passing heartbeat. Experimentally, I opened one eye to take a peak. My rack is where it's supposed to be, snug against the wall with the window on my left. The window, while geographically in the right spot, is considerably higher than where it should be meaning that my rack is lower to the ground then it should be, or my entire bed has sunk into the floor. While possible in the earthquake prone San Francisco Bay Area I dismiss this theory, figuring that an earthquake strong enough to make the floor sink would most likely have woken me up. My mind registers the changes and a shockwave of panic wakes me completely up.

I look around the room and realize that I wasn't in Kansas any more. Kansas being a metaphor for the cramped room I had called home for the past couple of years. There are other people asleep in the room, none of whom I know and I know everyone in my squadron. My mind starts to put the facts together. I'm definitely in a military barracks, one similar to the room I occupy so this must still be on base. There are people I don't know so this must be not be my barracks. I notice a set of dungarees and a Dixie cup (a term of endearment used by Navy personnel to describe their rather quaint little white hats). I'm on the Navy side.

"OH SHIT!", I think and probably said out loud as well, "I've been kidnapped by squids (a term of endearment Marines use to describe Sailors)." No soreness in my anal area, that's a major plus. No one seems intent on keeping me from leaving, also a plus. Of course, I don't see my clothes anywhere and was fairly certain that I had, in fact, gone to sleep in my own room. Now I'm only faced with the dilemma of figuring out where I'm at in relation to my own barracks and how to get from here to there in nothing but my skivvies.

I quietly extract myself from the bed and make my way to the door being sure that I wake no one, just on the outside chance that I was wrong about the whole kidnapping thing. I peek out into the hall and only two wings away I can see our duty desk. The hall is clear, I make a break for it.

157

By my own standards, I'm not a fast runner. I did do the 3-mile run on our bi-annual Physical Fitness Test in under 18 minutes (one second under but a 5.983333333333 minute mile isn't anything to complain about), but I'm not a great sprinter. Nonetheless, I must have had wings on my bare feet that day because I made my room in record time.

Imagine the look on my roommate's face when I barge through the door in nothing but my skivvies. His look of surprise and his question about where the hell had I been convinced me of his sincerity later when I asked about my experience with translocation. I grilled everyone in the barracks attempting to find out how I got from my own room to one two wings away with no knowledge of it occurring (I did once wake up in the women's barracks after a night of heavy drinking, next to a lady whose name I couldn't remember but at least I had some vague recollection of how I got there). I've never been known to sleep walk but that's a possibility. Outside of that, this is one for Unsolved Mysteries.

UNDERSTANDING

There's something to be said for having a girlfriend that truly understands your profession. With her being a police officer also, I don't have to switch languages and talk English instead of code when we discuss our days. There are different dialects in police work. For instance, My city and one of the neighboring jurisdictions uses one series of codes while most of the rest of law enforcement uses the 10-Code. They say 10-4 for acknowledge while we say 904 for the same thing; 10-20 is location and we say 926. But there's enough of an understanding that we don't have many problems and of course the penal codes, vehicle codes and health and safety codes remain the same so that when she calls me excited over a 11350(a) arrest, I understand exactly what she means. The understanding goes deeper than that though...

The other day we had received a complaint that one of our residents was involved in prostitution activity. The complainant, the suspect's brother, went so far as to provide pictures and a web site where she was peddling her wares. We had begun our investigation by checking out the web site we were given. Unfortunately, it wasn't a direct link and we had to spend some time going through various "possibles" while we sought the person we were looking for. As we're paging through various links, my girlfriend calls...

Me: "Hello."

Her: "Hello. What you up to?"

Me: "Surfing the internet looking for prostitutes."

Her: *laughs*

There is definitely something to be said for having a girlfriend that understands what you do for a living.

DUDE

One, among many, of my duties in the Department is to supervise the recruiting of police officer applicants. The selection process is long and includes a written examination, physical abilities test, oral interview, writing exercise, background investigation, polygraph exam, Chief's interview, and psychological, and medical exams. As long, and expensive, as the process is, I don't want to waste the Department's, or the applicant's time, or the tax-payers' money, on people who won't be a good fit for the Department or the community. Sometimes you don't find that out till the very end of the process, but, sometimes you find out before the process ever begins...

I was sitting in my office trying to clear some outstanding reports and prepping a background for one of my investigators. I generally leave the door to my office open so that my officers, other employees or citizens can come in and talk to me if they feel inclined to do so. On this particular day, my door was open. I was reading through the narrative of a police report and, out of the corner of my eye, saw someone enter my office. As I started to look up, I hear, "Hey, dude, where do I turn in my application?"

Looking up I see a man in his early 20's wearing the standard issue police academy uniform with the logo of the particular academy he attends embroidered clearly on his chest. My eyes narrow. My name and rank are neatly stamped into a name plate on the door as well as on my desk. I'm in uniform so only an idiot could miss the stipes on my sleeve. Citizens can call me whatever they choose and even when it's less then polite, I don't sweat it. My officers and fellow employees, as long as they're nice about it, have only a little less latitude depending on the tone of the conversation we're having. An academy cadet who applying for a job as three options, they can call me Sergeant, Sergeant Cotes or sir. In my days at the academy, everyone who wasn't wearing the light blue uniform shirt of a cadet was sir or ma'am.

Me: "You turn your application into me."

Cadet: "Oh, cool. Hey, do you have a copy machine around here? I need copies of my job history to put with my background packet."

Hmmm, no introductions. No, "Hi, my name is Cadet Dude and I'm applying to be a police officer with your agency." Nothing. My voice remains neutral.

Me: "There's a copy machine on the second floor. Stairs are to your left."

Cadet: "Oh, cool. Can you make copies of this for me?"

Now he's really beginning to impress me. Not only has he called me dude but he's walked into my office unprepared and wants me to stop what I'm doing and go make copies for him. Joy. My annoyance is rising. I know that a part of their training, especially as far along as this academy is, includes how this process all works. You're rated on everything. Every meeting you have with your prospective employer should be treated like the oral interview. You dress for the part, you act accordingly, you come prepared...

I decide that making him cry the first time he meets me would be bad for my recruiting efforts at his academy. He may be an inch away from being outright dismissed from the process but some of his academy mates might be good applicants and I don't want him bad mouthing my department and telling them that the "prick" of a sergeant that runs the process yelled at him. I take the papers he's holding out and go upstairs to give me a moment to get my ire under control.

I make the copies and go back to my office and hand them to him. He takes them without saying anything, rifles through them while I take a seat back behind my desk and adds a few to his background packet. When everything is organized, he grabs the stapler off my desk. It's the crappy stapler. I leave it on my desk so that if someone feels inclined to borrow it and forgets to return it, it's no big loss. The good stapler I keep in the drawer. He struggles with it and then sets it back on my desk.

162

Cadet: "Hey, it doesn't work." He waits expectantly.

In my mind, he's already failed out of the process. He has no survival instinct. He can't read the subtle signs that he's in danger. The knitted eye brows, the flushed face, the gritting teeth and clenched jaw. At this point, I'm not even convinced he would recognize more obvious signs that he's in danger, say something like, "F you cop, I'm going to kick your ass." I'm convinced he won't survive the streets of my rough and tumble city.

I take out the other stapler and hand it to him. He takes it without a word, rifles through the papers again and removes one. He crumples up that piece and puts it on my conference table. Once everything is organized he staples everything together and hands it to me with a "Here you go". I take and toss it on the floor next to my desk and then lean forward.

Me: "As the cover letter I attached to the application packet clearly explained that I would take your background package at the time of the interview, I want you to remind me that you have already given it to me. I'll probably forget who you are so when I conduct the oral interview I want you to remind me. Just tell me that you're the cadet that walked into my office, called me dude, was unprepared and had 'me' make copies for you and then left trash on my conference table. That should spark my memory."

The first dawning realization that he may have crossed a line somewhere in there starts to bloom on his face. Maybe I was wrong about his survival instincts. Maybe he would know to duck just seconds before the baseball bat hits him square across the forehead.

Cadet: "Ok. Will do." He smiles.

Scratch that last thought. He leaves. I pick up the application and break out a post-it and write one word across it before sticking it to the application. "Idiot."

NEW REGULATION

The Chief came down to line-up to swear in a new officer. Prior to the swearing in ceremony though the Chief noticed the two officers he had selected to grow goatees so that he could see what the goatees looked like in uniform before allowing us to grow them on duty. After less than a week, Brad's was coming in nicely and was exactly what the Chief had in mind. Ralph on the other hand only had a very small amount of hair on his chin.

Chief: That's not what I had in mind Ralph. I'm looking for a full goatee where the mustache flows into the goatee.

Ralph: I can't grow facial hair along the sides like that Chief. I can only grow a mustache and then hair on my chin.

Chief: Then I guess you won't have a goatee then.

Ralph: Come on Chief, I can't help it if I can't grow hair like that.

Chief: That's not what I had in mind. I want what Brad has. Yours doesn't qualify as a goatee.

Dave: Actually, what Brad has is a Van Dyke. Ralph's is more of a goatee.

Ralph: See Chief.

Chief: Then I want a "Van Dyke" and not a goatee. Go shave.

Ralph: Now?

Chief: Yes. Now.

Ralph: Come on Chief. I can't grow hair like that and I don't think I should be discriminated against because I can't grow hair on the sides.

Chief: That's not what I want so I guess you just won't have one then.

Ralph: Do we say that no one can grow a full head of hair because you have a bald spot?

I know the silence only lasted for a few seconds, punctuated by the occasional suppressed snickers, but it felt like a long time.

Chief: You have till Friday for me to see what it looks like.

I'm sure I'll be adding an addendum to policy here shortly regarding hair cut regulations...

HUGS

My fiancée' works patrol in a neighboring city. Prior to her and I dating, I would have told you that her city had some odd politics but was otherwise a quiet little college town. When we started dating, I found out differently. Her city is off the hook. At first I thought maybe it was my town's corrupting influence, it has always seemed to have more crime then is reasonably necessary and the idea was, that perhaps it was spilling over into neighboring jurisdictions. These days, I think that her city suffers from what so many of our cities suffer from, a lack of Darwinian intervention that has diluted the gene pool to the point that idiocy is a far too common occurrence.

Case in point. This evening she spots a pick-up truck driving erratically with no plates and the markings from the tow yard still etched in yellow chalk on the windshield. Her curiosity piqued, she does her duty as a law enforcement professional and conducts a vehicle enforcement stop. The driver is under the influence and probably would have blown a .08 had some other officers not performed a felony stop in close proximity to her vehicle stop and forced her and her perp to take cover as the other officers pointed their guns in their general direction while taking the suspect into custody. By the time that whole thing was straightened out, the driver only blows a .06. Under the legal limit for a DUI but good enough to earn him a few violations on a citation, a towed car for driving on a suspended license and the confiscation of his Remy Martin. As she takes the alcohol out of his car he asks if he can have it back. After all, he's already been cited for possession of an open container while driving so he feels it's his right to polish off the bottle. She tells him no. "What if I give you a hug?" He asks her. The answer is, of course, still no.

Well, the offer was thoughtful even if the execution would have landed him a nice, shiny pair of matching bracelets and an overnight stay in the fine accommodations at the City Jail.

I'M JUST FRIENDLY LIKE THAT

It was 2:30 am on a Saturday morning and I was on my way home from a 12-hour day at work. I like this time of night. First, I'm going home after a 12-hour day at work. Second, my city is peaceful at that time of night. My stereo was turned off; the police radio is quiet because all my officers have gone home. My window is rolled down and the only thing to break the silence is a quick serious of gunshots and the wail of a siren off in the far distance.

I'm stopped at a stoplight waiting for the green when an older model Toyota pulls in behind me. I glance up when the headlights hit my rearview mirror and see three occupants in the car. Their windows were down too, and I could hear their conversation clearly.

Driver: "Man, put it out. There's a cop in front of us."

Passenger 2 (from the backseat): "Man that ain't no cop. That's security or something. They're like patrol."

Side note: I drive an unmarked Ford Crown Victoria. It's not an undercover car and if you know what you're looking at, you can tell right away it's a police car. The blue lights are generally a giveaway. Other emergency vehicles driven by paramedics and fire have red lights but only law enforcement (in this state anyway) have the blue.

Driver: "Are you sure?"

Passenger 1: "Yeah. He's right. He isn't a cop. He can't do jack to us."

I look into my rearview mirror yet again and see them pass a lighted, cigarette type object from the rear passenger to the front passenger. I've never been a smoker, but I know based on my training and experience that people don't generally pass cigarettes around like that. Marijuana is a different story. Not sure what it is about weed that makes people think that putting your nasty lips in the same place that someone else just put their nasty lips is "cool", but they do.

The light turns green and as soon as we're through, they speed up, whip around me and as they drive by, they all wave and grin like fools. I smile and wave back. I'm friendly like that. As they make it past me I accelerate, move over in behind them and activate my lights.

There is this demented part of me that really, really wanted to be in that car when the red and blue lights flashed on and the siren cycled through. I could see the panicked scrambling around in the car but not the looks on their faces. I wanted to see the looks on their faces. Nonetheless, I did derive a certain amount of enjoyment out of the exaggerated attempts to fan the car's interior clear of the smoke.

Me: "I'm Sergeant Cotes with the Housing Authority Police. The reason I pulled you over was for changing lanes without signaling and for suspected involvement with drugs. As I can smell the marijuana, we'll skip the suspected part and get right down to you telling me where the rest of the weed is."

The occupants of the vehicle give me blanks looks. It's the kind of look that tells you that there is a whole lot of fantasy going on behind those eyes. You just know they're thinking, "If we ignore him, he will go away." I sigh.

Me: "Look, it's been a long day and I'm ready to go home. If you give me the weed, I'll give you a ticket and you'll be on your way. If I have to go looking for it, I'm going to take you all to jail and tow your ride."

There's some nervous wiggling around and then they start telling me where the weed is. They're not dealers. Just some low-grade users that thought a little marijuana on a Friday night, early Saturday morning was a good thing. I get two sacks, one from each of the passengers. Everyone gets a ticket and I'm back on my way to the PD to drop off the evidence.

As we get up to next light they've somehow ended up behind me. As they pull up, I smile and wave at them. I'm friendly like that. Funny that they didn't smile and wave back.

PRACTICAL JOKES

To keep myself entertained some days, I'd play practical jokes on people. One this particular day, I quickly typed up a list of instructions for our new, "voice activated microwave" and hung them up on the microwave that had been in the breakroom for several years.

Around lunch time, I was sitting in my office when I heard one of the officers say, "Microwave, On." When nothing happened, he repeated the command, only this time a bit louder. "Microwave! On!" Once again, when nothing happened, he said the command again even louder and when that failed to get the microwave to turn on, he started cussing.

He must have heard my hysterical laughter because the next thing I heard him say was, "Very funny Lieutenant."

Another time, I put a sign up near the stairs leading down to the 1st floor of the department that read, "Stairs Out of Order, Please Use Elevator." I found out later that one of the civilian staff had been using the elevator all day when she finally went down to where the Chief's administrative assistant sat and demanded to know when the stairs were going to be fixed.

My all-time favorite joke though, I purchased a tiny noise maker that was about the size of a quarter and had a magnet on the back. When turned on, it made a number of different noises including the wind blowing, a creaky door opening, the sound of a child laughing, and a spectral voice that said, "Can you hear me?" I placed it on the keyboard tray at my training assistant's desk.

An hour later, I walked by my assistant's desk only to have her flag me down, "Lieutenant," she said, "I think my desk is haunted." She was dead serious.

"What makes you say that Nancy?" I asked her.

"I keep hearing things. Noises and a voice that asks me if I can hear him."

I struggled to keep a straight face. "Probably just some program running in the background on your computer. I doubt it's haunted. Of course, there was that lady that died here."

"What lady?" She asked, with her eyes widening.

"I wouldn't worry about it." And I moved on with whatever it was I had been doing.

Not long after that, she flagged me down again. This time she had proof, having recorded once of the sounds on her cell phone. "You hear that? Right there!" She said as she played it back for me.

I clearly heard the voice she had recorded but claimed ignorance and told her that I was hard of hearing any way.

Two hours later I came back to find her no longer at her desk. She was down near where the Chief's administrative assistant's desk was, doing her work at the counter.

"Nancy, what are you doing?" I asked her once I had found her.

"My desk is haunted, I'm not going back."

I figured at this point, I had played this trick as far as I was willing to let it go. After all, I needed her at her desk so she could do her job. I told her I'd play around with her computer and see if I could figure out what was going on. Removing the noise maker, I proclaimed it was some program running in the background and that I had shut it down and she should be "ghost" free now.

She returned to her desk but I felt the whole joke had been so successful, I decided to try it on one of my sergeants and placed the noise maker in his office, attaching it by the magnet to the back of a wall locker he had. Truthfully, I got busy after that and forgot about it.

Later that day, I went to his office to ask him a question and walked in to find him with both hands in a death grip on his desk. He was bent over in his chair with his head underneath the desk saying, "I know you're in here. I can hear you." I started to lose my composure and, because he didn't know I was there, I simply walked away so I could have a good chuckle.

I returned about an hour later. This time I found that he had taken everything off his desk and everything out of his drawers. He was clearly agitated and, no longer able to contain myself, I started laughing.

I found out later that the device had him so worked up, he was threatening to initiate Internal Affairs complaints if someone didn't tell him where the sounds were coming from.

SARCASM

A friend of mine and I had just finished eating lunch and were standing outside the restaurant when a guy walks up and starts looking at his uniform.

Man: "Transit Police?"

My Partner: "Yes sir."

Man: "I didn't think you looked like a real police officer."

My Partner: "I didn't think you looked like a real asshole either but that doesn't mean it's not true."

SMART ASS PART 1

One day I got called in to the Sergeant's office.

Sergeant: "I'm talking to you because you're the POA (Police Officers' Association) president and the officers tell you things they don't tell me and I want to know who did this."

Me: "Ok. What happened?"

Sergeant: "Someone wiped a booger on the wall in the locker room next to the urinal. I want them found and I want them disciplined. It's a sign of a sick mind and we can't have that kind of sickness on our force."

Me: "Sarge, it's a booger."

Sergeant: "I know it's a booger god dammit. I want the booger DNA tested. Hell, I'll pay for it myself. And I want whoever put it there arrested."

Me: "Arrested for what Sarge?"

Sergeant: "For littering. Hell, I don't know, but I want them punished."

Me: "For a booger?"

Sergeant: "Who did it?"

Me: "I have no idea Sarge."

Sergeant: "They had to have been right handed because the booger is on the left and everyone knows you have to hold it with your strong hand when you piss. That or they can use both hands. So, I suppose they could be left handed."

Me: "You've put a lot of thought into this."

Sergeant: "It's gross."

Me: "That I know."

Sergeant: "It's the sign of a sick mind."

Me: "So you've said. But it's a booger Sarge. You don't want to pick this fight."

Sergeant: "You think this is funny don't you? You're a smart ass. Get out of my office."

SMART ASS PART 2

I was a resident police officer in one of the larger public housing complexes the east side. The other day I was going out to empty the litter box when I saw a van pull up and start to unload a bunch of garbage into our parking lot. I was wearing civvies so there was no reason to think I was a cop.

Me: "Sir, I know you're not going to dump that stuff here."

Man: "And why not?"

Me showing my badge: "Because I'm a Housing Authority police officer and this is my home."

Man looking at badge: "I guess not then."

Me: "See, that's what I like. A man with a brain between his ears that can see reason when it stares him in the face."

Man: "You're a smart ass aren't you?"

Me: "I've been accused of that a time or two."

OVERHEARD ON THE RADIO

1 6L6: "It's in his pants right in front."

16L8: "Where?"

16L6: "In his pants. Just reach in and grab it."

16L8: "You just want me to reach down the front of his pants and pull it out?"

16L6: "Yeah. Just reach down there and yank it out. You should be able to get your hands on it."

16L8: "What if I can't get my hands on it."

16L6: "Oh come on. If you have to, pull down his pants and grab it."

Sergeant: "16L8, get the drugs out of the guys pants."

16L8: *snickers* "Aye, aye Sarge. Already done."

You could almost hear the realization dawn on him.

16L6: "You're going to pay for that Kev."

MORE PRACTICAL JOKES

After running rear ending a car, one of our officers became so flustered that when he tried to pull off to the side of the street he hit a Snapple delivery truck. By the time he got back to the station, his entire wall locker was plastered with Snapple stickers.

That same officer was exiting the freeway and collided with the cement guard rail. In his statement he said that "a small furry animal" had ran out in front of him and had he hit it, his wife would have divorced him. By the end of the next day we had a beautiful certificate naming him PETA's Man of the Year.

One of my trainees happened to be a personal friend of my sergeant. At the beginning and end of every shift, I have my trainees check the patrol car to ensure that no contraband had been secreted while we had a subject sitting back there. At the end of one particular shift, my trainee checked the back of the patrol car and pulled out what appeared to be a wrapped kilo of cocaine. I was pissed that we had somehow missed someone dropping a kilo and wondering how the heck I was going to explain that to the sergeant. As I'm sitting there trying to (less than) calmly explain this to my trainee, he has the audacity to suggest that we just throw it away. My (less than) calm demeanor dropped and I proceeded to explain the consequences of destroying evidence, especially that much evidence. We head up to the sergeant's office with me dreading having to explain this.

My sergeant is not as calm as I was in dealing with this. It's 2 am in the morning and he wants to get home to his wife and kids and because of my incompetence as a Field Training Officer my rookie had missed an entire kilo. He told me we were going to have to call the

DEA and they were going to want to interview us and that I might as well call my wife and tell her that I wasn't going to be home until 6 or 7 in the morning.

My wife (now ex-wife) was an unreasonable and very disagreeable person. I dreaded calling her to tell her I was late more than I had dreaded telling the sergeant about the kilo. I was on the phone a matter of seconds before I was being accused of lying and cheating and just wanting to go drinking with the "boys".

I have a great rest of the evening to look forward to. I get to hear more lectures from the sergeant, I get to explain to a federal agent how I let my trainee miss an entire kilo of cocaine and when I get home, I get to argue with my wife.

By the time I get back to the sergeant's office, my trainee has convinced him to give up on the joke (he was a smart man and knew he had to ride with me for the next several weeks and that I filled out his evals). It was all a set up. My trainee had borrowed the "kilo" from a friend of his at the DEA who used it as a training aid. My sergeant had been in on it.

My ex-wife however didn't believe me and thought I came home early because I was feeling guilty about lying to her. And people thought I had a cruel sense of humor.

SERGEANT'S OFFICE

Getting called into the Sergeant's office without an explanation is probably one of the most stressful moments in an officer's day. A hundred things run through your head. You're trying to figure out who you pissed off, what you did wrong, what you did wrong that could get you in serious trouble. Sometimes I like to get on the radio and have an officer come to my office just to mess with them. One day I picked on Joey.

Joey: "You wanted to see me Sarge?"

Me, typing away on my computer and not looking up: "Close the door and sit down."

Joey closes the door and has a seat on the other side of my desk. I continue to type for a few minutes dragging the tension out.

Me: "How do you spell negligence?"

Joey: "N-E-G-L-I-G-E-N-C-E"

I continue to type for another couple of lines.

Me: "How do you spell terminate?"

There's silence from Joey so I finally glance up and see that he's sweating profusely.

Me: "Oh, this doesn't have anything to do with you, I just called you in to see how you're doing."

Joey breathing a huge sigh of relief: "Damn you had me scared."

EVEN MORE PRACTICAL JOKES

When I was an officer with the municipality, I had a lieutenant that liked to drive up on us when we were stopping large groups of people and drop firecrackers, the really loud kind, just to see everyone duck and run for cover.

One night we staged a fictional foot chase for an officer. His partner intentionally left the car unlocked. While the two of them were in the back of the property chasing a fictional suspect, Tom and I rolled down all the windows in the patrol car and then spread some broken glass we had found all around the car. When the officer and his partner returned, he thought all his car windows had been broke out. He did the right thing and called the sergeant. The sergeant comes out (consequently, we forgot to include him in on the joke) and stares at the car and starts cursing up a storm. "How am I going to explain this to the Chief?" Tom suggests that if we can get it fixed tonight the Chief would never have to know. "Tom," says the sergeant, "it's 1 in the morning, if you can figure out how to fix those windows tonight I'll give you tomorrow off." Tom sits down and smugly rolled up the windows.

Another fun one with new dispatchers...

Me: 16L75 can I get a trip on a roller? (license plate check on a moving car).

Dispatch: 16L75 go ahead.

Me: It will be 7 Mary, Mary, Mary, One, Two, Three

Dispatch: 16L75 it comes back clear and current to a 1999 Honda registered to a.....hey that's my car.

Me: 16L75 go again?

Dispatch: 16L75 that's my car. No one should be driving it. Any units for cover on a 10851 (stolen car)? 16L75 what's your location?

Me: I'm out at 2020 20th Avenue (the address of the station).

Dispatch: Oh. You're joking right? Please tell me you were joking.

CONCLUSION

As a young Marine who entered boot camp at 17, I never would have imagined my life taking the path that it did. Since the age of 8, I had it set in my mind that I was going to be a Marine and it was going to be my career. After my first enlistment, I was bored of chasing wires on aircraft and, after the Marines told me they wouldn't let me do anything else, needed something more challenging. At 20 ½ years old, I applied for my police job and was hired.

Not quite 3 years after that, I ended up working for my department and it has been a fun ride. I have served everywhere from patrol to SWAT. I stepped down from my position as a Lieutenant and the Commander of Field and Special Operations less than a year ago now. I have worked with some of the very best people in law enforcement and I have worked with some people I thought should never where a badge. It has had its ups and its downs, but I am ultimately proud of the work I did, and I will always love the city I worked in and her people, no matter how dysfunctional they may sometimes be.

Thirty-one years after I stepped off that bus in San Diego and onto the yellow foot prints at the Marine Corps Recruit Depot, I'm still a Marine at heart but now I where a different military uniform, that of a Chief Petty Officer in the United States Navy Reserve, that I am equally proud of. I have hung up my police uniform and turned in my badge and gun. The girl friend I refer to in some of my stories, I ended up marrying. She still works in law enforcement and is a sergeant for a jurisdiction that neighbors my city. Dexter the Wonder Dog is pushing 22 years old and it is starting to show. Age catches up to us all.

Thank you for taking the time to read my book. I'm hoping my new career as an author and semi-professional adventurer will be as successful as my last two careers have been. If you find the book worthy, share with your friends and family. If you're curious, follow my page on Facebook or my Instagram at wayne.cotes. I also have my own website at www.waynecoats.com and please, feel free to leave comment on Amazon or Goodreads. Good or bad, they help.

Semper Fi.

CPSIA information can be obtained
at www.ICGtesting.com
Printed in the USA
BVHW031122060423
661868BV00007B/288

9 781649 089021